WHO MINISTERS TO MINISTERS' WIVES

... AND EVERY OTHER MISUNDERSTOOD WOMAN?

Helping the misunderstood Christian woman

find her place in a culture she doesn't understand

INCLUDES A 1993 INTERVIEW WITH DR. BEVERLY LAHAYE

Libby Seamans

Copyright 2019 by Libby A. Seamans. All rights reserved.

Printed in the United States of America. No part of this book may be used or reproduced in any manner whatsoever without written permission from the publisher.

For information, address Family Tree Publishing, 2419 S. Venice Drive, Pearland, TX 77581

Family Tree books may be purchased for educational, business, or sales promotional use.

FIRST EDITION

Library of Congress Cataloging-in-Publication Data has been applied for.

ISBN – 13: 978-0-9851328-2-8

SUBJECTS – Women | Discipleship | Christian Life | Holy Spirit

All scripture quotations (*unless notated*) are taken from the Holy Bible, New King James version Copyright 1982 by Thomas Nelson, Inc. Used by permission. All rights reserved.

Scripture taken from the New American Standard Bible (NASB), Copyright© 1960, 1962, 1963, 1968, 1971, 1972, 1973 1975, 1977, 1995 by The Lockman Foundation All rights reserved Used by permission. http://www.Lockman.org

This book is dedicated to –

The faithful ministers' wives who tirelessly support the furtherance of the gospel...

Dr. Beverly LaHaye, whose efforts with Concerned Women for America (CWA) preserved the voice of Christian women and the Biblical values for which we stand...

And to those who never let go of my hand–those who walked the walk with me:

Kathy Bear-Carlson (1987)

Starla Bridges (1990)

Valerie Murphey (1992)

Dianne Clearman (2001)

Rosilyn (Roz) Houston (2005)

Special thanks to JoAnna Alcorn and Cynthia Rodriguez for the tireless hours spent editing and for their endless encouragement to keep going.

Contents

INTRODUCTION 5

Chapter One – A CALL TO SERVICE 11

Chapter Two – THE MINISTER WITHIN 29

Chapter Three – GETTING PAST THE PRESENT 44

Chapter Four – DIE TO SELF, OR SELF-DESTRUCT 73

Chapter Five – LIVING ABOVE THE CIRCUMSTANCES 87

Chapter Six – CODEPENDENT ON CHRIST 101

Chapter Seven – A SOUND MIND 116

Chapter Eight – YIELDED, BUT NOT FORGOTTEN 139

Chapter Nine – MEET BEVERLY LAHAYE 154

Chapter Ten – MAKE THE TRADE 163

References 172

Changing Lives With Truth in Story 173

INTRODUCTION

In general, to say women are misunderstood is an understatement. To say Christian women are misunderstood is a grave understatement––and the minister's wife, well, she is perhaps the most misunderstood. Why do we feel this way? Do we bring it on ourselves? Is it because we're irrational? Emotional? Aloof? Gregarious? Overdressed? Underdressed? Strong? Smart? Speak out? *Right, my thoughts exactly*. There seems to be no end of reasons why we are misunderstood. Whether in the House of Congress or the White House, in the board room or on the church platform, or cooking in the kitchen with a baby on our hips, we are judged. And unfortunately, often the judging comes from women and men alike within the church who just don't understand us. Of course, we are judged by a modern-day society distorted by a culture that we no longer comprehend—a culture where we must fight for the very right to surrender to a life lived for Christ. All this judging and misunderstanding can sure weigh us down. It can stop us in our tracks. It can stop us from doing the very thing that God has ordained for us to do. What can we do? You've probably said, like I have, "They just don't understand me. I'm doing my best to live for God. I'm trying to hear His voice. I can't meet all the expectations. I can't please everyone." Ladies, we *can't* please everyone, and if we try, we may soon feel

INTRODUCTION

like we can't please *anyone. Stop worrying about pleasing everyone. Determine to please God.*

Trust me, just as sure as we have a big win, just when something we put our hand to is successful...here comes the criticism. *You shouldn't be standing up and speaking out. You should be hosting a garden party, not a political party. You shouldn't be working--you should be home taking care of your family. You shouldn't be on the platform Sunday morning—women are supposed to keep silent in the church.* And, from the opposing side: *You should pursue what makes you happy —don't surrender your dreams to make your husband happy. You sacrifice enough—don't submit to the demands of a selfish man*...and on it goes. Either way seems to be the wrong way. What can we do? Where can we go when the heaviness settles in around us? When condemnation is crushing us? Who can we talk to without ruining our witness? Do we keep smiling and saying we're fine? No...well, maybe. *"And having done all, to stand, stand firm."* Remember that one? It is there for a reason. Don't let life knock you over! **Don't let Satan knock you out...let him bring you to your knees. It is there, on your knees, where you make your stand.**

"For to me, to live is Christ, and to die is gain." Philippians 1:21

The words Paul wrote could be entertained by any of us at any time. After all, 2 Corinthians 5:8 says, *"We are confident, yes, well pleased rather to be absent from the body and to be present with the Lord."* The problem with this thought, of course, is that our desire to be "absent from the body" may well have a different meaning than Paul's did. Perhaps you've considered that it would be better to die and be with Christ? I have. What a relief it would be to not have to go through another hopeless, discouraging, debilitating circumstance, another rejection, another disappointment, another day of living under the weight of guilt and condemnation, another day of not being loved, another day of not measuring up. Your life is so hard, and you are so misunderstood that you feel you cannot face another day? Been there.

Fortunately, this was not what Paul meant. Paul wasn't saying *he couldn't* go on. He simply knew that to be present with the Lord Jesus Christ would be so much better than to live here with the inevitable day-to-day trials, beatings, hunger, and, yes, the frustrations, disappointments, and deep heartache of ministering to the church. Of course, if you continue reading that passage, you'll see that Paul chose to live on. He chose to live on for the sake of the many, for the sake of his witness, for the sake of those who needed to hear the gospel. Paul understood that his life was going to be lived purely as a witness and testimony to bring others to the knowledge of salvation. So, how did he press on with that kind of understanding? How was he able to go from day to day knowing that his life would be a living sacrifice, to be lived not for himself, but for the

INTRODUCTION

sake of others? *He would have to die to self so Christ could live through him.* Locked in chains, witnessing to his fellow prisoners, he once proclaimed, *"But the word of God is not chained."* 2 Timothy 2:9. There was no prison that could hold the truth. He was chained for a reason—to proclaim liberty to men who were in chains—to proclaim liberty to those of us who are in chains. His chains fell, and the doors swung open…and so can ours.

Perhaps your husband has stopped fulfilling his ministry to you and your family because of the demands of his calling, whether as a full-time minister or full-time provider. Or maybe you're the full-time provider, you're single, or you're a single mom, and you are alone, trudging through life just trying to survive. Or you may be on the front lines of ministry or the front page of the political debate, dodging the fiery darts of social media. You find yourself crying out to God, "Oh Lord, I can't do this on my own." FINALLY! *He has been waiting to hear that. You can't do it on your own.*

In March of 1992, the Lord spoke to me just as clearly as I am speaking to you. This is what He said: *"Today I am calling you out. I am calling you out to be a light. I am calling you out to proclaim the truth. I am calling you out to tell them I have not forsaken them. They are not alone. Do not be afraid. My provision will go with you."* I believe it is God's calling for my life to tell you that God has not forsaken you, to speak to your heart the things He has spoken to my heart, to proclaim to you the truth about who God is and how that truth will set you free, and to demonstrate to you that no matter how hopeless things seem, no matter how forsaken you feel, or how alone, or how much in despair, He has not forgotten you. He has not left you alone. And for those of you who know these truths already, those who have walked the walk for twenty, thirty, or fifty years, it is my calling to encourage you to share these truths with others, to wake you up, so you, too, can lead the way. I am living proof of the power of God to change lives, and so are you.

There is someone who ministers to me in the darkest night when my husband, Frank, is a thousand miles away, or just miles away in his mind. I am not alone, and neither are you.

As a pastor's wife, perhaps you're about to break under the feelings of isolation. The pain of sacrifice has gotten to be too much to bear. Or as a traveling evangelist's wife, you're slowly dying from loneliness as your husband goes away for weeks at a time. Or as a wife of a husband so consumed with making a living, he forgets to live, your losing your desire to live. Or as a woman on the front lines of politics, 24/7, social media harassment is about to crush you. Or, perhaps, you're the only woman in the boardroom, a misunderstood woman who feels like you just don't fit in. Whatever the circumstance, IT is stealing your joy or, rather, Satan is stealing your joy. He knows if he takes your joy, he takes your strength.

Just maybe, there have been nights you sat up in bed, when the tears wouldn't subside, and you cried out from the depths of your

INTRODUCTION

heart, "What about me, God, who will minister to me?" *and then felt guilty about that.* Hold on. *It is time to put a stop to the lies. There is more. God has more for you.*

It is extremely difficult to guard against our natural emotional responses once in a state of vulnerability, so our best defense against Satan's attempts to destroy us, our families, and our ministry, *is to prevent it from ever happening*, like taking preventive medicine, inoculating ourselves from the infection. But, if we do succumb to the infectious lies and snares of Satan, don't fear. There is an antidote. I believe with all my heart that the revelations God has given me were intended to do just that. So, get in line, make a fist, and prepare to be inoculated with the understanding that—God sees you where you are, has called you for a specific work, and has given you the gifts and power to fulfill that call. AND, this understanding is intended to be an antidote for anyone who has or will fall prey to Satan's infectious lies and snares.

The truth is, God's Word says, "Therefore, if anyone *is* in Christ, *he is* a new creation; old things have passed away; behold, all things have become new." 2 Corinthians 5:17. Are you living like all things have become new? You can. That very revelation should put a fire in you. It has me.

Chapter One – A Call to Service

Prior to my marriage to Frank, I spent five long years as a single mom with two small sons who knew well what being alone was. I was in my mid-twenties. I knew well what being misunderstood felt like. I knew well the harsh judgment of others. I was the divorcee who didn't fit with the singles group, where the well-meaning mothers told their sons to steer clear of me. I didn't fit in with the young married group, where the innocent young wives shunned me, too afraid for their husbands to be around me. I didn't expect to feel alone again. I didn't expect to find myself not fitting in again…but it was happening. I was married but felt like I was single again.

Twenty-nine years ago—just a few years before I wrote this book, and then tucked it away—in my early years of marriage, I was hit with the reality that my sweet, wonderful Frank was not just "my" Frank anymore. The man the Lord had given me, the companion of my dreams, the one I had been praying for, wasn't just mine. After a short time of having him all to myself, *well, except for our five sons*, something was going wrong. He started giving himself to someone else. I don't mean another woman, thank God. Instead, he was devoting his all to saving a lost and dying world. He was becoming completely consumed with the calling God had placed on his life to minister to others, and as a result, he was neglecting his ministry to our family, and he didn't even realize it. Once again, I was alone with my sons, only now I had five.

Let me stop here for a minute and challenge you to see others through the eyes of Jesus—the one who knows the torment and torture that assault each of us every day in our fight against Satan—and look with compassion and grace on how you can lift them up and welcome them in. You'll never know who they are or how they may impact your life, or how you could impact their lives, if you dismiss them, if you shun them. After all, did Jesus look like the Redeemer when He was born, lying in poverty, in a manger? No. Most didn't recognize Him. Some still don't recognize Him. Many shunned Him. He didn't fit in. He didn't fit the mold. Don't let preconceived notions cause you to miss the one sent to be your miracle or miss the one for whom you are supposed to be a miracle. Don't judge. Their hearts ache for someone to care. Haven't you ever felt like you didn't fit in? That you were misunderstood? Perhaps you wear a good façade; everything on the outside looks perfect, but the inside is a mess. A little self-evaluation usually reveals the logs in our eyes. If you need understanding, be understanding.

Now back to my story.

Shortly after Frank surrendered to the call of full-time ministry, our lives began to change. Not as if we needed any more change. Barely in our thirties, living with yours, mine, and ours, change had become our new normal. But this much change? We were not prepared. I was not prepared. As Frank searched for God's will, he became more and more involved in church activities. He joined the choir, headed up an outreach committee, taught a Sunday School class, and volunteered for a plethora of other ministry efforts. He was blessed with so many talents, not the least of which was the ability to stir your soul with a song. His pitch-perfect anointed singing was a gift and tool that God would use.

However, all these new commitments and responsibilities demanded more and more of his time. With his relentless quest to find his place of service, the place God had ordained for him, I found he had little time for us. I withdrew from the things I had been involved in. The boys needed one parent at home they could count on. I didn't resent it...*or did I?* I wholeheartedly felt it was important for Frank to pursue God's will. I loved seeing him so dedicated to seeking God's calling, whatever that was. I was ready. I had it all. Prior to our marriage, I had prayed for many years for a godly husband who would not only be the spiritual leader of our family, but one who would tell my sons about the "birds and bees." Now I know that might sound a little silly, but I did pray that the Lord would send them a father before they reached the age of asking about girls. I didn't know how I would navigate that one. And after five long years of praying, I had him, and, I might add, his two sons as well—adorable two-year-old twins. Wow! Now, add Frank Jr., in our first year of marriage...I really did have it all. On top of that, Frank was the best-looking man on the planet. How could I say a word about a few hours without him? Well, as it turned out, I didn't say anything about the time spent alone. *It was much worse than that.*

I'm not sure when I took the bait. Satan lured me in with little wormy negative thoughts at first, then he hooked me. I desired God with all my heart, yet my thoughts were far from Him. On the one hand, I loved seeing Frank, a new Christian, mature into a new creation, seeing the carnal desires replaced with spiritual desires, seeing anger and discontent replaced with peace and excitement about what the future held. On the other hand, I was afraid he would spiritually outgrow me. I hate to admit it, but I found myself envying his spiritual growth, if you can believe that. I should have recognized Satan's trap. I didn't. I became jealous of his Christian relationships, and even jealous of his relationship with God. All the things I had yearned for him to become were becoming a threat to me. God had given me everything I had asked for in a husband, and then some, and was now asking me to give him up. I knew the feelings I was experiencing were not from God. I knew nothing good could come from my envy and jealousy, but there it was.

1 Peter 2:1-2 tells us, *"Therefore, laying aside all malice, all deceit, hypocrisy, envy, and all evil speaking, as newborn babes, desire the pure milk of the word"* and Titus 3:3-5 says, *"For we also once were foolish ourselves, disobedient, deceived, enslaved to*

various lusts and pleasures, spending our life in malice and envy, hateful, hating one another. But when the kindness of God our Savior and His love for mankind appeared, He saved us, not on the basis of deeds which we have done in righteousness, but according to His mercy, by the washing of regeneration and renewing by the Holy Spirit." Why was I experiencing such ugly thoughts? Satan had seen my weakness and gone for the jugular. I just thought I knew who I was in Christ, but when tested, I failed. I hated how I felt and prayed earnestly for God to create a new heart in me, to help me see things the way He sees them. And He did just that. He began showing me that my ways were clearly not His ways. If I was going to survive, I would need His wisdom. I would not be able to withstand the attack using my own understanding. At the time, I didn't even realize it was an attack. I didn't understand spiritual battles. All I knew was how I felt, and I didn't like it.

James 3:16-17 makes it clear: *"For where envy and self-seeking exist, confusion and every evil thing are there. But the wisdom that is from above is first pure, then peaceable, gentle, willing to yield, full of mercy and good fruits, without partiality and without hypocrisy."*

Now, all you "mature" Christian women might be ready to put the book down but stay with me. You haven't heard it all. Well, maybe you have, but you didn't like what you heard. It seemed one-sided; it's not. It's God-sided! He calls us all to heed His Word. You are responsible to Him, just like I am. He says to seek Him first and all things will be added, and I have found this to be true. Jesus has spit on the ground and made a salve for your eyes. With his anointing, *read*, and you will see.

When my eyes were opened, I realized I had been blinded by my self-pity. I repented. When I was tempted to go down that path, I asked God for help. When I felt like I was getting the short end of things, I ran to God. I denounced the harmful feelings. No matter how I felt, I surrendered everything, and every time, the Spirit strengthened me. I knew the only thing that really mattered were the souls of men and glorifying God. I desired with everything in me to become the woman God wanted me to be. I yielded to Him. That was what He was waiting for.

The first thing God desires of us is to be willing and yielded. Before He could use me, I had to surrender my hurting heart. I had to surrender what I thought would make me happy, to experience true happiness. To be strengthened by His joy, I had to let go of my joy.

To receive what I'm going to share with you, you must lay down your will and yield to His. If our eyes are blinded by jealousy, we can't see the path. If our hearts are hardened, we will miss Him. We will miss the very thing we desire.

Lay the book down and pray that if there is any bitterness, or envy, or jealousies, or anger, or *anything at all* that would hinder you from hearing the truth of His word, that you would put it aside and open your heart to whatever God wants to say to you. So, in the end, you can say, "I see."

Now—let's move on.

Submission and obedience are two words synonymous with women. Although the world, or, dare I say, the Christian world, and perhaps our own husbands, may have taken those two words out of context and twisted them to mean something altogether different than what the Lord intended, it remains true: we are to submit and obey. Don't tune me out now. I am a woman, not a man secretly trying to dupe you. As you'll see by the time you get to the end of the book, God is not a God of inequality but of equality. If we will fully surrender and walk in obedience to His Word and do what He requires of us, He will greatly reward us. There is freedom in surrender. There is strength in surrender. There is peace in surrender.

Surrender and obedience are not new concepts. God allowed the children of Israel to be taken captive to teach them obedience. He knew that their true salvation—real freedom—would only come through obedience to His instructions. His laws would keep them safe. They would have to trust Him. He knew that only through obedience and trust would they find rest. He did it because He loved them. He teaches us obedience because He loves us. But if we allow our circumstances to harden our hearts and close our ears like it did theirs, we will never be free. We will never be free of the chains of anger and resentment and envy and bitterness if we can't hear the voice of the Holy Spirit—the very One sent to teach us all things, to convict us of sin, and to lead us to freedom. When we shut down to the ministry of the Holy Spirit, we are on our own. We *are* alone, and that is not what God intended. We were never meant to be orphaned. He will do what He must do to bring us to safety…to bring *you* to safety. To freedom.

~~~~~~~~

Have you ever felt like you were talking to a brick wall when having a confrontation with your child, or, dare I say, with your husband? Or maybe when talking to someone with a different political view? Or, should I say, especially when confronting someone with a different political view? Have you felt like they didn't hear one thing you said? Well, guess what? They didn't hear a word you said. When a child is in rebellion or a husband or opponent shuts down to your opinion, it doesn't matter how hard you try to get through, how much sense you make, how loudly you talk, they cannot hear you. It is the same with us. Once we allow ourselves to walk in obstinance and disobedience, there is a wedge put between us and the Holy Spirit. Not only can we not understand what He is saying, we reach a point where we can no longer hear what He is saying. If we can't hear His voice, we can't receive His ministry. We lose out on all He was meant to be for us. If you want to survive this side of heaven, obedience is a must.

Deuteronomy chapter 8 is the best instruction on obedience that I know of:

"Every commandment which I command you today you must be careful to observe, that you may live and multiply, and go in and possess the land of which the LORD swore to your fathers. ²And you shall remember that the LORD your God led you all the way these forty years in the wilderness, to humble you and test you, to know what was in your heart, whether you would keep His commandments or not. ³So He humbled you, allowed you to hunger, and fed you with manna which you did not know nor did your fathers know, that He might make you know that man shall not live by bread alone; but man lives by every word that proceeds from the mouth of the LORD. ⁴Your garments did not wear out on you, nor did your foot swell these forty years. ⁵You should know in your heart that as a man chastens his son, so the LORD your God chastens you.

⁶Therefore you shall keep the commandments of the LORD your God, to walk in His ways and to fear Him. ⁷For the LORD your God is bringing you into a good land, a land of brooks of water, of fountains and springs, that flow out of valleys and hills; ⁸a land of wheat and barley, of vines and fig trees and pomegranates, a land of olive oil and honey; ⁹a land in which you will eat bread without scarcity, in which you will lack nothing; a land whose stones are iron and out of whose hills you can dig copper. ¹⁰When you have eaten and are full, then you shall bless the LORD your God for the good land which He has given you.

[11]Beware that you do not forget the LORD your God by not keeping His commandments, His judgments, and His statutes which I command you today, [12]lest—when you have eaten and are full, and have built beautiful houses and dwell in them; [13]and when your herds and your flocks multiply, and your silver and your gold are multiplied, and all that you have is multiplied; [14]when your heart is lifted up, and you forget the LORD your God who brought you out of the land of Egypt, from the house of bondage; [15]who led you through that great and terrible wilderness, in which were fiery serpents and scorpions and thirsty land where there was no water; who brought water for you out of the flinty rock; [16]who fed you in the wilderness with manna, which your fathers did not know, that He might humble you and that He might test you, to do you good in the end— [17]then you say in your heart, 'My power and the might of my hand have gained me this wealth.'

[18]And you shall remember the LORD your God, for it is He who gives you power to get wealth, that He may establish His covenant which He swore to your fathers, as it is this day. [19]Then it shall be, if you by any means forget the LORD your God, and follow other gods, and serve them and worship them, I testify against you this day that you shall surely perish. [20]As the nations which the LORD

destroys before you, so you shall perish, because you would not be obedient to the voice of the LORD your God."

Scary, right? Well, not if you remain obedient…not if you have no other gods before Him…not if you remain humble…not if you do not sit yourself in His seat. The rewards will be great for the one who obeys. Even though hard testing comes, stay the course. Some of you may be saying right now that you don't have a problem with being disobedient. You've submitted in every way to God's leading. You've submitted to your husband's calling; you've submitted to your position in life. *Really?* Have you ever considered that entertaining jealousy is being disobedient? Jealousy of your husband's ministry or the people he ministers to? Jealousy of your friend's perfect family? Jealousy that someone else got the promotion? *You know we will never admit it.* Unfortunately, jealousy is a natural human emotion, especially jealousy of a woman that poses a threat. We women are ready to pounce at the first sign of a threat. But, be very cautious. Before you make any judgements, ask yourself: Is the threat real or imagined? Are your thoughts based on facts or are they based on feelings? Jealousy is an in-road for Satan and must always be guarded against. Remember the love chapter, 1 Corinthians 13:4: "Love is patient, love is kind and is not jealous; love does not brag and is not arrogant." (NASB) Satan is out to destroy your relationships, and that includes your marriage. When jealousy starts to creep in, ask God to reveal the truth and protect you and the other person from this destructive emotion. Jealousy stems from not trusting. Don't misunderstand me, I do believe we should be on our guard. I do believe we should pray for our marriage and our friendships daily, but once we pray, we must trust God. If we don't, we open the door to anxiety, false accusations, and anger. You see what I mean? Living with jealousy is living in disobedience. Believe me, I understand that struggle; I've lived it. Take it to God before it destroys you. Ask God to give you confidence and peace concerning your relationships, knowing He sees all. Pray diligently that He will guard your marriage and your mate against any tactic Satan tries to use. Once you put jealousy aside and walk in confidence, people will be drawn to you. Your husband will desire to be around you more. No one is drawn to a fragile, weak, negative person. *That's not you!* Of course, there will be times of illness, and sadness, and even moments of feeling inadequate, and your husband and friends *will* come to your side in those times. I'm talking about being in a place of *sustained* weakness, jealousy, and negativity. No one wants to be around that person. You know it's true. It brings us down. We turn and go the other way when we see *that* person coming. And the good news is—we don't have to be that person! God has declared we are more than conquerors! So, get up. Get into His Word and don't take the bait! If something is going on, God will reveal it.

Proverbs 31 tells us that wisdom will bring health and vitality, restoring our youth. One could say God's wisdom lived out in our lives is the very fountain of youth. *We do live forever, you know.* So, drink freely. Our Father will equip and empower us as His favored daughters to carry out the plan He has destined for us. It may not be the plan we have envisioned, but trust me, it is the best plan. Let me tell you my story.

I relayed earlier that Frank was quite talented, and that talent was what propelled him into the spotlight. One of his first opportunities to be used for God was to portray Jesus in an Easter cantata. Finally, he would have a chance to show others what God had done.

After weeks of rehearsals, the evening for the performance had arrived. I took my seat in the second row. The church was at capacity. My mind pondered the possibilities for the evening; perhaps many would get saved. The lights dimmed as a faint chorus of "Hosanna" was heard over the hushed crowd. A spotlight drew our attention to the back of the sanctuary. With long hair, a full beard, and a flowing white robe, *Jesus* came riding in on a donkey.

Hosanna, Hosanna. The donkey moved slowly down the aisle, past the crowd, past me…Jesus was in our midst. Stopping at the altar, Frank dismounted the donkey and began embracing the people with the love and compassion of Jesus through scenes of healing and forgiveness. Everyone was captivated, transported back to the time when Jesus walked the earth.

A CALL TO SERVICE

That donkey that had made such a grand entrance, left standing at the front of the sanctuary, decided he needed to go, and I don't mean leave the room. Right there in front of God and everybody, the donkey did "his business"! It was the biggest pile of donkey dung I had ever seen...not that I had seen a lot of piles of donkey dung. Once I collected myself from the initial shock and disgust, I remembered the next scene was the crucifixion. Jesus would give way to the burden of the cross right in that very spot. The impact of the moment would be lost. The message would be lost. And perhaps the appointed time of salvation for a ready soul would be lost. I had to do *something*. I had to clean it up. The tugging on my heart compelled me. The Holy Spirit would not let up. I had to obey.

While the lights were down, I hurried off to the kitchen to find a box to put it in. (Yes, it would take a box.) After making my way back up the aisle, there in the shadows, I got down on my knees and began scooping the fresh donkey dung into the box. Affronted by the awful smell, I could hardly breathe. I could hardly keep from gagging. I tried holding my breath, only to gasp, forcing gulps of disgust into my lungs. There was no escape.

Then, a rush of unexpected joy flooded over me, my face flushed with warmth as I wept in silence. *What was happening*? I was overwhelmed. In an instant, in that very strange moment in time, I was changed. The Most High God called me by name. He spoke to me and called me into service:

"Libby, this is what I have called you to do. You will be in the shadows cleaning up the mess. You will do the hard part, the part no one will see."

Trembling, my tears unconstrained, I finished scooping up that donkey dung there in the shadows. I wasn't crying because of what God said I had to do, I was crying because He had counted me faithful to do it. I was crying because God had looked down upon that whole congregation and saw me…chose me. I was crying out of a grateful heart. At that very moment, He was calling me into service, into a life of serving. He had called my name, and I had heard Him.

I didn't realize the full impact that calling would have on my life, on the life of my family, or on the life of my husband and the ministry he would soon be called into. I did know that I had come to a point of full surrender, a point of complete yielding of my heart for the cause of Christ. The point we must all get to.

Just as Isaiah had said, *"Here am I, send me."* I, too, was willing to do whatever God wanted me to do and go wherever He wanted me to go. I was willing to seek the profit of the many that they might be saved. If my heart had not been yielded, I would not have heard His voice; I would have missed out on the call that God had for my life. Philippians 2:3 says, *"Let nothing be done through selfish ambition or conceit, but in lowliness of mind let each esteem others better than himself."* That night I had not considered what people might think or how dirty the job was; I simply esteemed others more highly than myself and responded. This is what God's Word says we should do, we *must* do. However, hear me on this: it was not in my own self that I did it. It was by the grace of God. It was by His Spirit. It is the righteousness of Christ in us that produces any good work. Let everything be done for the glory of God.

We must be ready to do the lowliest of jobs. By its very definition, lowly means "humble in manner and spirit, free from self-assertive pride."(1) James 4:6 tells us "God resists the proud but gives grace to the humble." *This is the second requirement for being used of God: to have a heart of humility.* We cannot pick and choose our calling, or our giftings. We haven't the knowledge or the wisdom. God alone has the knowledge and sovereign authority to appoint our places of service. It is His Spirit that gives gifts according to His purpose and pleasure.

I finished cleaning up the mess and quietly went back to my seat. Just like the blind man who received his sight after washing the mud from his eyes in the pool, my tears washed the mud from my eyes. I could see.

Just like in the days of old, God had used a donkey to bring about His will. Unknown to me, that night my Father prepared me for the plans He had for me. The full effects of that night were still unseen. My encounter with Him would last a lifetime. Tears still flow as I write and recount that night when God saw me and called my name.

You may not have the most desirable place of service or receive man's recognition, but ours is of a higher calling. Ours is to do the will of the Father. The things of this world have no hold on us. I want to leave you with this thought: **When God calls us to a place of service, He does not leave us powerless. If He calls us, He will prepare us and equip us.**

I recall in the late 90s, when Frank first met Joel Osteen, his brother-in-law, Gary Simmons, was giving Frank a tour of the Lakewood facilities. Frank was recording a project for Gary and there was some discussion of a potential place for him at Lakewood. During the tour, Gary introduced him to Joel. At the time, Joel was producing the weekly televised programming for the church. He passed by this meek, obscure young man who simply looked up briefly to say hello, his eyes barely visible from beneath the baseball cap. Later when we heard that Joel would replace his dad as senior pastor at Lakewood, we could hardly believe it. We fully expected Gary to step into that position. Gary was very dynamic and poised and capable. We just couldn't imagine Joel filling his daddy's shoes. Boy, were we wrong.

1 Samuel 16:13 says, "Then Samuel took the horn of oil and anointed him in the midst of his brothers and the Spirit of the Lord came mightily upon David from that day forward." In Acts 13:22,

A CALL TO SERVICE

"...and when He had removed him, He raised up for them David as king, to whom also He gave testimony and said, 'I have found David the son of Jesse, a man after my own heart, who will do all My will.'"

God will never put us in a place of service without equipping us, without anointing us, without empowering us to perform the task He has set before us. David was a lowly sheep herder, but God anointed him to be a king. Joel was an obscure man, but God brought him out of obscurity and anointed him to proclaim His Word. God saw him beneath the baseball cap. God saw his heart for Him. Joel was hidden in the shadows, obscure to man...but not to God. God willed him into the spotlight to be a powerful presence for Him.

If you are willing to humble yourself before the Lord, He will exalt you. If you are willing to step out of the shadows, or step into the shadows, lay aside your pride, your jealousies, your envies, your hurts, *your fears*, and put yourself completely in the hands of our Savior and Lord, He will not disappoint you. He can use you. He will use you!

Proclaim today, *"I am a woman full of His Spirit. I have understanding, and I will not waste it."*

"May He grant you according to your heart's desire and fulfill all your purposes." Psalm 20:4

Chapter Two – The Minister Within

The first thing I want you to know is: ***You are not alone.*** I have talked with countless women and have been amazed at how many times I've heard the same story. The story of feeling isolated and alone, abandoned by the one you trusted. "How could this happen?" you ask. Well, it's simple. It's Satan. The scripture tells us that Satan is out *"to steal, kill, and destroy."* That is his purpose. He hates God's creation. He hates that he can no longer lay claim to man because man has been redeemed. He looks for a weakness, any weakness, then carries out his attack in subtle, crafty ways—many times through something or someone we would never expect. I have considered his strategies and schemes over the past thirty years as I've witnessed ministers becoming so busy doing God's work that they neglected the important things in their own home. Be on your guard. Don't let this happen. I believe Satan will literally use the calling on your husband's life to pull him away from you—whether it's—the calling to full-time ministry or full-time provider. Both are noble. He will then use the ensuing loneliness, confusion, and pain to cause bitterness between you and your husband, and then between you and God. Satan's plot is to destroy the family and ultimately ruin your ministry and your witness. Don't let him!

I've also seen *and experienced* the isolation and despair of being a single mom, rejected by those who profess the love of Christ. She walks away from God. She walks away—from potential—from power—from being a witness to other singles or even to her own children.

Sadly enough, Satan's plot is finding success. The reason for its effectiveness is that Satan's strategies are so subtle that damaging feelings begin to grow without being noticed. The gaping hole in your heart just appears without warning. One day you wake up and find yourself feeling alone and isolated. You feel as though everything you do or say is misunderstood, and you don't know how or when it happened. I'll tell you when it happens. It happens anytime we get out of balance, anytime we lose the proper perspective—God's perspective. You see, Satan continually strives to redirect our focus from God. If he can overload us with commitments at our jobs, with kids, finances, not to mention the church, and a myriad of other commitments–—until our focus is ON US, he has us. We will become so self-absorbed with our life, we don't see anyone else, and we don't hear anyone else. Eventually, we no longer hear God. Satan's end game is to lull us into despair, to lull us into sin, to lull us into a catatonic stupor so we have no voice. Instead of being a witness that benefits the Kingdom, our witness damages the Kingdom. The ministry meant to unite families could divide and separate them. A failed marriage can mean a failed ministry, perhaps damaging the potential of every seed that was planted. Whether your husband is a full-time minister or layman with a heart to minister, Satan has the victory. Whether you're a woman leading a singles ministry, or a single mom ministering to your family, when you withdraw, when you walk away, Satan wins.

That's the second thing I want you to know: ***What you are experiencing is an attack of Satan.*** It is his scheming that brings about the separation, the isolation, and the despair.

For those of us who are married, Satan will even use the praise and recognition God may grant our husband to cause envy and jealousy to stir in our heart. While we labor sacrificially behind the scenes, he stands in the spotlight, basking in the accolades of man. Just as easily, we can become jealous of those receiving his attention and devotion, maybe to the point of resentment. As his mate, we deserve his best…and we're getting his worst. Others are getting his undivided attention; we are getting his frustrations and exhaustion. We may even begin to question his love. A spark in our imagination sets our minds ablaze. In our many hours spent alone, we wrestle with thoughts of infidelity. After all, where is he all the hours he spends away? We no longer find worth in our labor and begin to believe the *lie* that our role is menial and unimportant. *What's it all for?* we ask. Exhausted with the struggle, eventually, we give up. We lose heart. Satan's ultimate victory comes when he plants a seed of rebellion in our hearts at our point of despair, so we begin rejecting God and the comfort of the Holy Spirit. *Now* he has us.

I have no way of knowing what your situation is. I know that not all ministers' wives are in a state of despair or that not all Christian women lead a hopeless, lonely existence. Of course we don't. But if you've experienced *any* of these emotions, I can imagine you feel as though there is no one you can turn to. You don't want anyone to know. After all, you're supposed to be submissive and supportive, a woman totally yielded to God's plan, totally trusting in God's provision—and all the other things people expect you to be. *All the things we should be*. Who are you going to talk to? You certainly don't want to bring your husband's character or ministry into question. You certainly don't want others to think God isn't big enough to take care of your problems. So, who is going to hear your cry? Who is going to minister to you? It can be a painful and desolate place to be. I want you to know there is someone to talk to. There is someone who wants to minister to you. Don't give up. The very thing you desire is at hand.

The third thing I want you to know: ***We have every right to expect companionship.*** That is how God designed us. God looked at man and declared it was not good for him to be alone. That is what the institution of marriage is all about. So, before we go any further, cast away any self-condemnation you may be feeling. Desiring companionship isn't wrong. It's only wrong when we desire another's companionship more than we desire companionship with God. Satan is so crafty. If he can't crush us with jealousy, he will crush us with condemnation. He will make us feel guilty for having the very desires we were designed to have. He will use our natural human emotions against us. If you are feeling condemned in your desire for your husband, or your desire *for a husband*—don't. You are being lied to. God's design is perfect; it is Satan who corrupts it. It is Satan who manipulates God's Word just enough to cause confusion, just enough to cause us to question our natural desire for love and companionship. Jealousy is bad; a pure healthy desire for a mate is not. The desire for companionship is not a selfish desire.

Now that we've identified the enemy and understand his crafty tactics, we can begin to fight back effectively. But know this: The fight is bigger than we think. We will not win it on our own. We can only stand against Satan through the power of the Holy Spirit.

"And I will pray the Father, and He will give you another Helper, that He may abide with you forever—the Spirit of truth, whom the world cannot receive, because it neither sees Him nor

knows Him; but you know Him, for He dwells with you and will be in you." John 14:16-17

God knows that we can do nothing in our own strength. Psalm 103:13-14 says, *"Just as a father has compassion on his children, so the Lord has compassion on those who fear Him. For He Himself knows our frame. He is mindful that we are but dust."* (NASB)

When God breathed the first breath of life into Adam, He knew then what His children would need. Man's future failures were no surprise to Him. We would need His Spirit. And by His Spirit, every provision would be made—the answer to every question, the strength for every battle, the comfort for every hurt, the light to show the way.

"But the Helper, the Holy Spirit, whom the Father will send in My name, He will teach you all things, and bring to your remembrance all things that I said to you." John 14:26

"The Spirit of the LORD shall rest upon Him, the Spirit of wisdom and understanding, the Spirit of counsel and might, the Spirit of knowledge and of the fear of the LORD. Isaiah 11:2

"Nevertheless, I tell you the truth. It is to your advantage that I go away; for if I do not go away, the Helper will not come to you; but if I depart, I will send Him to you." John 16:7

The Holy Spirit is *the minister within*. He is our comforter, our helper, and the one who teaches us all things.

We have all heard throughout our Christian walk that the Holy Spirit will bring us comfort. Maybe you've heard it so often you are sick of hearing it because you don't feel comforted. I don't know where you stand, but from the time God called me into this life of serving—there on my knees scooping up that donkey dung—until today, *thirty years later, as a pastor's wife*, I have not found anyone who can comfort me like the Holy Spirit. The Holy Spirit comforts with a deep comfort that pain cannot penetrate.

We can't feel Him, and we can't see Him, but He is there just the same. Always there. The Holy Spirit has been the one to minister to me throughout all these years. He has taught me the truths that make me strong. He has given me a sound mind. He has shown me the way when I was lost. He calmed my fears in the raging storms. Yes, the Holy Spirit is our minister within. He is the one who gives understanding to the misunderstood woman.

When we get rid of the barriers that stand between us and the Holy Spirit, we will receive His ministry—the ministry that is the secret to our survival. All the strength and power we need to live victoriously in this crazy world ***is inside of us***, although one might certainly think it is a secret by the looks of things.

Why else would the Church be so diminished? Based on the nightly news, the current culture represents the very opposite of Biblical values, yet 68% of Americans identify as Christians (2). Why would the Christian divorce rate be over 30%? (3) *We are not walking in the power of the Holy Spirit.*

We long for power; we yearn for it, strive for it, and cry for it, and all the while, it's inside of us: the power to overcome, the power to have hope in a hopeless world, the power to live in peace amid chaos and confusion, the power to love instead of hate.

In John 14:12-14, our Lord says, *"Most assuredly, I say to you, he who believes in Me, the works that I do he will do also; and greater works than these he will do, because I go to My Father. And whatever you ask in My name, that I will do, that the Father may be glorified in the Son. If you ask anything in My name, I will do it. If you love me, you will keep my commandments."*

Wow! How much clearer could it be? What a promise! Those who believe will have the power to do greater works than Jesus. How? By calling on Jesus' name. Why? That the Father may be glorified in the Son. *Nothing about this promise has changed!*

What are the greater works? There has been much debate and many sermons pontificating answers to that question.

Generally, the works of healing, prophecy, and signs and wonders are the usual ones offered up, but I believe there is more to it than the supernatural works of signs and wonders. I am no scholar, just a woman offering another thought. Consider 1 Corinthians 13, the "Love Chapter". *Could it be that the attributes and demonstrations of love by millions of Christians are the greater works?* The kind of love spoken of in chapter 13 can only be acted out through the power of the Holy Spirit. It's the same power that enabled Jesus, as He hung on the cross, to look to the Father and say, *"Father, forgive them, for they do not know what they do."* The power to love unconditionally—not accepting someone's sin, but, like Jesus, loving them while they are still in it. The power to release all the abuse and shame and pain to our Heavenly Father and love even our enemies the way Christ loved—the way we want to be loved—the power to say, **"Let me rise above who I am and demonstrate who You are."**

Only by the realization of GRACE through the ministry of the Holy Spirit can we rise above our sin…our guilt…our shame, to love the way Christ loved. We must receive it to give it away. We must experience His work in us to do the works.

The Apostle Paul could never have overcome the shame and guilt of killing so many Christians if he had not grasped the fullness of grace. Not only did he overcome the guilt of his past, but he did the greater works. He loved the enemy who beat him and bound him in chains. Paul didn't care about hurt feelings or a bloody back; he cared about saving souls. In distress and in persecution, with peril on every side, he plotted his missionary journeys, knowing that going could mean his death. The founding of the early church and the salvation of thousands happened because a man took Jesus at His word. *The world needs us to take Jesus at His word.*

My heart's cry is to unfold a pure and complete understanding of that grace and the supernatural strength and fortitude that comes from having an intimate relationship with Jesus. The acceptance of grace will enable you, as it did Paul, as it did me, to overcome the barriers of past failures and of present circumstance and propel you forward with the freedom to love the way Christ loved. Can you think of a greater work? A love that is patient and kind, a love that isn't jealous or arrogant, or easily provoked. A love that *never remembers a wrong suffered.* Now when was the last time you didn't remember a wrong suffered amid your pain and in your despair? Are you living out a love that hopes all things, a love that endures all things? *A love that never fails.* Now *that* is a work to strive for. And the truth is, we are all equipped to do it. By the power of the Holy Spirit, we can love like Christ loved, with a love that never fails.

As women, as wives of ministers, as ministers, we must open the lines of communication between us and the Holy Spirit and walk in that kind of power and that kind of love. For those of you who already are…AMEN!! For the rest of us, we need to figure out why we are not.

Why are we not living in the power and privilege and provision of the fullness of the Holy Spirit every day, all the time? Why are we not living a life of peace? Why are we not loving the way Christ loved? Could it be we're not meeting the conditions? Yes, the reason we walk in the weakness of the flesh and not in the power of the Spirit is that *we are not meeting the conditions.*

To fully receive the ministry of the Holy Spirit, we must have *unwavering faith.* I know you've heard it a thousand times, but remember: Without faith, we cannot receive from God. Without faith we cannot please God.

James 1:6-8 *"But let him ask in faith, with no doubting, for he who doubts is like a wave of the sea driven and tossed by the wind. For let not that man suppose that he will receive anything from the Lord, he is a double-minded man, unstable in all his ways."*

Hebrews 11:6 *"But without faith it is impossible to please Him, for he who comes to God must believe that He is, and that He is a rewarder of those who diligently seek Him."*

We must believe that God is and that He is a rewarder of those who diligently seek Him. The very definition of faith is *"the substance of things hoped for, the evidence of things not seen."* We must see the things we hope for through spiritual eyes of faith. I know it isn't easy to see if your eyes are swollen shut from crying. It isn't easy to be certain you will receive the things hoped for if your hope has evaporated. I get it. I've lived it. So how do we get back to that place—the place of hopeful expectation? The place of knowing that God's Word, His promises, are true, even for us? Even for you? Look, listen, and learn. Pry your eyes open. Take out the earplugs you put in to silence the pain. Open that little sliver of heart you have left and open your mind one more time to the possibilities. Now drink in everything God has for you.

ACTION PLAN:

LOOK at the place the Lord has brought you from.

LISTEN to the experiences of others. Go to a ladies meeting and hear the testimony of someone who has made it, someone who was delivered from a hopeless situation. Read about someone else's victory.

LEARN about the love of God—the love of God that keeps us going and the love of God that draws us back. *Learn* about His nature and character. Pick up His Word and start reading. Analyze the actions of the apostles. Ponder the paths of Ruth and Esther and Mary Magdalene. Take apart the life of Abraham or Peter, bit by bit. See what made them different. Why did Peter take that first step on the water? Why did Mary run to tell the others that she had seen the resurrected Jesus? FAITH! *They believed*. They trusted in what they had seen and what He had said. They trusted in who He was.

MEDITATE on every word. Growing your faith is like growing a strong, healthy body. You need to learn what it takes to keep it strong and then do it. Sound too basic? It's not. If you neglect to nourish and exercise your body, you will end up a weak, frail heap on the floor. You don't want to be a heap on the floor. Faith works the same way. You cannot neglect it; you must exercise and nourish it.

DECLARE a fresh start. Put a plan in place. We need structure or it won't happen. Like the first day of exercise, it might be hard, but it gets easier with every trip to the gym.

Day One of your new regimen: *Feed* your faith. Remember and make a list of experiences that required great personal faith that ended in victory. You *do* have some. You may have to move the baggage off the top, but they are there. Before everyone piled on all the stuff, burying your faith, crushing your hope at the bottom, it was there; it's still there. Keep digging.

Tap into the experiences of others. Attend meetings, read books, have one-on-one conversations, listen and learn about victorious testimonies. Schedule it on your calendar. Set aside time to read no matter how early you must get up or how late you must stay up.

See, I said it would get easier. Now, *exercise* your faith. ACT. Work on your attitude by doing good works. Good works produce joy. Little by little, as your joy grows, your soul is nourished, which strengthens your resolve, which creates fertile ground for your faith to grow. Start with smaller weights, little acts of faith. God will move, His Word says He will, and He is not a God who would lie. *S-T-R-E-T-C-H*. Believe in something big. God will move, His Word says He will. Repeat. Continue this exercise regimen for as long as needed. Now, reach for the unreachable. Lay hold of that vision and go for it. Walk in certainty, with conviction. All things are possible with God. Instead of crying out for a miracle, walk like you already have it.

Why is it easier for us to believe in the miracle of salvation, and walk in it, than to believe He will provide food for the day? Or that He can restore love to a broken relationship, or that He can save your child? When we doubt His ability to bring these things about, we are saying, *"Lord, you are not enough."* He **IS** enough!

Remember, no negative thoughts. Have nothing to do with them! Anxiety, doubt, worry…those are for the weaklings. Take those thoughts captive. We are strong. We are more than conquerors. We're bodybuilders. Our bulging muscles of faith make it evident to those around us that we are spiritually fit! When I see a bodybuilder, I see determination and discipline. I know because I know what it takes. I was one *many* years ago. And so it is with our faith. As we grow our faith by examining what God's Word says about our life, or our situation—healing for our bodies, financial provision, restored relationships, peace of mind—and believe, seeing His promises fulfilled, we become faith powerlifters and God is well pleased. He will pour out immeasurable blessings…immeasurable power to do the greater works.

So, lessons learned:

– Don't allow doubt to block the blessing of communicating with God through the Holy Spirit. A mustard seed of faith will unleash His power. We will move mountains.

– Don't allow a bag of emotional trash to bury your faith. Empty it the minute it comes in. Toss out the lies with the garbage.

As we allow the Holy Spirit to minister to us, we will see a miraculous transformation in ourselves, in our relationships, and in our marriages. So, open your hearts and receive the ministry of the Minister within. We will love so profusely it will surprise us.

"In the day when I cried out, You answered me, And made me bold with strength in my soul." Psalm 138:3

Chapter Three – GETTING PAST THE PRESENT

Have you ever suffered with debilitating depression or gasped for breath from uncontrollable anxiety? Have you been paralyzed with fear when hearing your child has cancer? Worried where your next meal would come from? Panicked when the power was turned off and you had no money to turn it back on? Or simply struggled and fretted over the demands of everyday life? Of course, you have. Whether mountain or molehill, at some level, we all get trapped in this snare—the snare of worry, and fear, and anxiety. You know it is not God's plan. Right? In fact, it displeases Him. We've all heard it said that we need to get past our past, and there are countless seminars and self-help programs designed to help us overcome some damaging incident in our past. But what about getting past the present? I'm talking about seeing past our present circumstances, our present heartache, and seeing good on the other side. How is it possible to look past the mess we're in and see something good? It's called HOPE. Having hope is simply believing that something good is going to happen. Let's face it. There are a lot of times when it looks as though there is no good thing in sight. Let me tell you about one of those times.

One evening I was preparing dinner when my thirteen-year-old son Jason came down the stairs crying uncontrollably. The pure terror in his eyes broke me. *Oh, God, what is wrong with my son?* Once again, I had been called to pick him up early from school because of a debilitating headache and vomiting, which had happened several times over the past few weeks. He looked at me and said, "Mom, I feel like a bomb is going off in my head." I asked him if he needed to go to the emergency room, and, to my surprise, he said yes. Now my Jason was the toughest, most adventuresome thirteen-year-old on the planet. I knew it was critical if he wanted to go to the hospital. He was the healthy kid who never got sick—the kid who played every sport—the one who leaped over tall buildings in a single bound. You know the kid I'm talking about. That kid. My heart sank. I headed up stairs and helped him get ready. While waiting to see the doctor, I called our church and let them know what was happening and added him to the prayer chain. I knew those faithful warriors would lift him up. At the time, Frank was singing with a group called *The Sound*, and, as fate would have it, was several hundred miles away and couldn't be reached. I called the group's assistant and asked her to try to locate Frank and let him know we were at the hospital. (The world without cell phones…imagine that.)

Finally, we were called back to the exam room, and I related how Jason had started having headaches and vomiting a few weeks back, but that today his headache had become unbearable. I saw his tears mingle with fear as they started IV fluids and announced they would do a CAT scan of his brain as a precaution. The attending physician told me Jason would need to stay the night because of his severe dehydration and they would advise me in an hour or so of the results of the scan, but… no one advised me of anything. They moved us to a room. The phone rang around 1:30 am. It was Frank. With a steady voice, I filled him in and told him to call back in the morning when I would know more. He didn't need my fear; he would have his own. We prayed.

Jason was feeling better the next morning, joking that he must have a brain tumor since no one had come to tell us the results of the scan. About that time, the doctor walked in. You might have guessed it. With a very grim and solemn look, he explained that the CAT scan had revealed a four-inch mass on the back of Jason's brain and that he had arranged for an ambulance to take us to Texas Children's Hospital. There was no time to waste. A team of doctors had been alerted and was waiting for him there. The best neurosurgeon in Texas would be handling his case.

I walked over to my Jason as the tears washed over his desperate face, and, with all the conviction I could muster, I said, "Jason, Christ did not give us the spirit of fear, but of love and power and a sound mind, so we are going to cast away any fear, and we are going to rely on Christ. He created you and He can heal you." I clutched his trembling hand and we prayed. I assured him I would not leave his side until it was over.

There had never been a time in my life that I desired more to be past the present circumstance and on the other side than during that ride to Texas Children's in the ambulance with lights flashing and sirens screaming and my Jason on the brink of death. I prayed and cried to the Lord, desperately longing for Frank to be with me. I wanted Jason to have the strong arm and love of his father to hold onto, but I knew he wouldn't get home for another four days. I told the Lord that I would trust Him to fulfill the need, and He did. The medics pushed the gurney through the open door, and there waiting for us was our youth minister, a strong man of God whom Jason trusted. Scott was God's provision.

The doctor proceeded to tell me that there wasn't much hope for Jason. He said he could die at any moment, or if he didn't die, he could become blind or a paraplegic. They would operate Friday morning…in four days. Frank was in a small town somewhere in Texas and had no way to fly home. I had told him to do his Wednesday night concert and then head for the hospital. You can imagine the pain he felt...the condemnation he felt for not being with us. He stood on the stage that night hopeless and helpless and told 2500 people about our son and asked for prayer.

Frank arrived home on Thursday. Determined to fight through the fear, we locked hands and prayed through the night. Friday morning our pastor, Kendall Bridges, showed up early to encourage us before surgery. He said he would be hosting the *Praise the Lord* program on TBN that morning and would ask all the viewers to pray.

The nurse led us back to where Jason had been prepped for surgery. His head was shaved, and he was slightly sedated. We stood around his bed gazing down at him, pretending that we weren't worried, but unable to mask our fear of losing him. He saw right through us.

Jason looked up at his dad and said, "Don't worry, Dad. I know when I open my eyes, I will either see you or I will see Jesus. I am not afraid."

We were stunned! We had no words. In that moment, our young, innocent son became a giant. His dependence on Christ was sure. He was able to see past the present and know that *whatever* the outcome was, good was on the other side.

Sometimes we can't see good because we have predetermined what good is. Jason, in his innocence, rested in God's determination of good.

The news of Jason's dire condition spread quickly throughout the gospel music industry. At the time of his surgery, literally thousands of people across the globe were praying. We were all believing for something good.

The surgery that was supposed to take eight to ten hours, was over in two. The doctor was visibly perplexed but glad to deliver the news. He removed the *cyst* and Jason would be fine. A condition that should have left him dead or critically impaired had been totally eradicated without any adverse effects. The doctor had told us that, at the very least, operating that close to the cranial nerve would most likely damage the nerves in his face, leaving him disfigured and unable to speak properly. But, in fact, *nothing* the doctor had prepared us for came to pass. Jason was completely whole…completely healed! He just celebrated his 40th birthday.

If I had not had my hope firmly in Jesus Christ and His promises, I would have fallen apart. God kept me when Frank wasn't there, but He did more than that. He sent Scott to be the answer to my prayer. He provided for that specific need I had asked for—a strong, godly man in whom Jason trusted, to stand with him. Tragedy had struck, and it looked like there was no good thing in sight, but our faith and trust in God allowed us to see past the present circumstance and have hope to believe in something good on the other side. What Satan meant for evil, God used for good. Our family had been a witness of strength and courage to everyone on the seventh floor of Texas Children's Hospital...and to the thousands who were praying. They had witnessed the power of God and rejoiced in it with us.

I suspect at some time in your life you have ministered to a parent with a desperately sick child, or perhaps to someone who is terminally ill, and found that, even though they were not a professing Christian, almost invariably they turned to God, whoever He is, and asked for help. At that critical point, during a devastating situation, even those who say they are nonbelievers will pray that there is a God who can rescue them, heal them, heal their child, save them—a God who can give them reason to hope. Let's show them there *is* reason to hope.

Another good thing that God gave me through all of that was a dear and lasting friendship. Jason's best friend's mother, Valerie, a beautiful woman of God, would befriend a stranger and gain a friend for life. Her son Matt told her about Jason, and the morning after we had been transferred to Texas Children's Hospital, she showed up with a bag of necessities, knowing I had not left the hospital since the night we went to the Emergency Room—a change of clothes, toothbrush, and toothpaste, and other items that made it possible for me to stay at the hospital and not leave Jason's side. This woman whom I had never met, met me at my darkest hour. We remain close friends to this day, twenty-seven years later, and have walked with each other through many dark hours and many new dawns.

There may be a time, or many times, when tragedy strikes, and you are all alone. You may feel like God and everyone else has deserted you. When that happens, remember this story—the story of my Jason. It was four days before Frank could get home to us—four days that my son's life hung in the balance. Hold onto your faith. Hold onto the truth. Hold on to hope. Let his story be an encouragement to you. Know that God will see you through to the other side. He has something good in store. Like my Jason said, he would either see his dad or see Jesus. Either outcome was good. You can have hope—hope in the fact that our Father loves us and wants the best for us. Don't surrender to the world's way of thinking. Some said, "Frank should have been there for you, for Jason. He shouldn't have been away doing what he was doing." The world would have condemned him for leaving us alone all the time. Some did. Some tried to influence me into thinking that I shouldn't have to go through times like that alone. But I say to the world—to Satan—I am not alone. There is someone who always stands with me, and my hope is in Him. My hope is in my heavenly Father–

–the Father who said, *"I will never leave you nor forsake you."* It is His strength, His provision, that sees me through every situation, and He will see you through yours.

Let me take you back in time, back to the time of the great exodus of the children of Israel from Egypt, their exodus from four hundred years of bondage. God literally brought them out with great signs and wonders. It was a time of meeting with God face to face. I expect you have heard it said, or perhaps said it yourself, that if I had seen those kinds of miracles, I could believe God for anything, too. It would be easy to have hope during a tough time and live for Christ no matter what kind of opposition I was facing. Who couldn't have faith if they had seen a staff turn into a snake or a sea parted down the middle? *I don't know if we should be so quick to make that proclamation.*

What does it really take for us to believe, for us to take hold of God's promises and allow them to propel us past our present circumstance? Apparently, it takes a lot, for we continue just like the children of Israel—walking in unbelief, grumbling, complaining, and sometimes doubting the very existence of God. Okay, maybe I'm not talking about you, but *a whole nation did.*

If we read chapters 7 through 11 of Exodus concerning the plagues brought against Egypt because Pharaoh wouldn't let the people go, it's hard to understand how the Israelites ever questioned God and His ability to provide for them. How could they ever question His love for them? God even told the children of Israel what the plan was. Deuteronomy 7:1-2 says, *"When the Lord your God brings you into the land which you go to possess, and has cast out many nations before you, the Hittites and the Girgashites and the Amorites and the Canaanites and the Perizzites and the Hivites and the Jebusites, seven nations greater and mightier than you, and when the Lord your God delivers them over to you, you shall conquer them and utterly destroy them. You shall make no covenant with them nor show mercy to them."* He goes on to give them instructions on what to do once they enter the Promised Land and He has given their enemies into their hands. He tells them ahead of time what is going to happen: He is going to deliver them from their enemies and give them the Promised Land! So, what else does God have to do for them to believe? What else does He have to do for us to believe? He has told us what is going to happen. He is going to deliver us.

Look with me in Exodus 13:17: *"Then it came to pass, when Pharaoh had let the people go, that God did not lead them by way of the land of the Philistines, although that was near; for God said, 'Lest perhaps the people change their minds when they see war, and return to Egypt.'"* Do you understand what this is saying? God knew that they were not ready for battle; they were too weak—they didn't have the heart for it. So, He didn't take them by the way of the Philistines where He knew they would encounter war before they were ready. He knew they would become fearful and turn back. His desire was to bring them into a place of rest and freedom. He didn't want them to go back into a life of bondage. God knew just what they could take and just what they needed. Are you seeing my point yet? God will not take us into a battle that we cannot win. He will not put us into a battle before we are ready. If you are in a battle, you can believe that God is there with you and that you can overcome. You *will* overcome. God foretold the victory. God is the victory. He led them in a way that was safe, and He will only lead us in a way that is safe. Now, I didn't say there wouldn't be opposition, nor did I say it would be without testing. They would certainly be tested; that was all part of His plan. In Exodus 16:4 and Deuteronomy 8:2, God tells them that the reason they were led through the wilderness, the reason their only food was the manna that fell from heaven, was to test them to know where their hearts were. He wanted to know what they were made of. He wanted to know their level of faith. We are tested for the same reasons. God needs to know where we stand with Him. Didn't He test Abraham to the point of sacrificing his own son? God provided the sacrifice when Abraham demonstrated his trust in the provision before he saw it. God didn't forsake

Abraham, He never forsook the children of Israel, and He will never forsake us. Remember the story how He guided them with the pillar of fire by night and a cloud by day, and His miraculous provision of shoes and clothing that never wore out? And what about manna falling from the sky and water pouring out of a rock? You see what I mean? During their dismal and dangerous journey, in what seemed like a hopeless circumstance, His provision *never* failed. **Every day He brought them closer to their blessing.**

They knew He was leading them into the Promised Land, for they had witnessed the signs and wonders that caused Pharaoh to let them go. There should have never been a doubt about God's presence or provision. There should have never been a question about God's great delivering power to deliver them completely—just like we should never question the power of the blood of Jesus to bring about our deliverance, our cleansing, our salvation. But they did question. And, I dare say, so do we.

After the awesome display of God's power and provision, the Israelites once again became fearful and doubted God. We see in Exodus 15 that just three days after the parting of the Red Sea—where it looked as though they would surely die, but God led them safely to the other side—just three days after He drowned the enemy that was pursuing them—they once again bitterly complained and longed to go back to Egypt. Grumbling, complaining, worry, and distrust were constant in Israel's camp. Are they constant in your camp?

~~~~~~~~~

Stop fighting against where God has you…you are preventing Him from giving you the very thing you desire!

~~~~~~~~~

The people complained because they didn't have water. So, God gave them water and satisfied their thirst. They got tired of the manna and complained about that. Every time God responded to their need with miraculous provision, a new need would arise, and they again complained and became fearful and unbelieving. They had no faith in a God who had proven His faithfulness. I don't know about you, but there have been times in my life that I prayed for manna when the plates were empty, and God sent us a bag of groceries. But the next time they were empty, I became afraid again. Our first year of marriage found us both unemployed with four boys and expecting our fifth. Many evenings I set a bowl of chicken and dumplings in front of them and then explained that Dad and I weren't hungry. I weighed less when I delivered than when I got pregnant, but Frank Jr. was born strong and healthy at eight pounds four ounces. I figured it out…*eventually*. Praise God.

We see miracles every day, and we have the same promises, yet we don't have the faith to see past our circumstances and believe for the good, believe God. We allow fear to grip us just like it gripped them.

Let me share another story about an everyday miracle, a miracle where my obedience to the prompting of the Holy Spirit kept my son from running away from home. My Jason had been having some struggles, temptations, and frustrations, and they were being manifested in some intense conflicts at home. His grades began to drop, and with each correction, his resentment grew, and his grades got worse. It was a vicious cycle. One day the Holy Spirit prompted me to pick Jason up from school and take him to lunch. I didn't really want to, but I knew God was telling me to do it. At that time, he was on restriction and had not been able to go out with his friends. We were not on good terms. I went to the school unannounced and, to Jason's dismay, asked him if he would like to go to lunch. I'm sure he thought the worst. While at lunch, I told Jason a story. It went like this:

A dad told his son not to do a certain thing again or he would be punished. He told his son that if he did do it again, he would have to sleep in the attic all night. Well, his son did do it, and the dad had to do what he had said. That night, the dad sat at the kitchen table with his wife, very distraught over the severity of his little boy's punishment. He wished he had never suggested such a punishment. His heart was breaking with the thought of his young son being in the dark attic, alone and afraid.

After a while, the dad rose from his chair and headed out of the kitchen. His wife asked where he was going, and he simply replied, "I'm going to sleep in the attic."

I told Jason that was what lunch was about. I had to stand with the punishment I had given because he had done wrong but that I wanted him to know that I was there with him in it. I would "sleep in the attic with him." I would love him through his confinement.

When I got home, I went to get Jason's laundry from his room, only to find all his clothes neatly packed in his suitcase. All his personal treasures had been bundled together for his planned departure. Who knew what was in his heart that brought him to the point of wanting to leave home? I don't know. But I do know this—it was the Holy Spirit who thwarted his plans. The love that I showed Jason that day changed his mind. I couldn't have known what he was about to do, but the Holy Spirit knew.

The next day, I went to Jason's room and found his clothes folded neatly in his drawers, his little treasures once again prominently displayed on his dresser. Gratitude flowed down my face. Praise God! I had walked in the Spirit and not the flesh. I had been angry with Jason and hadn't really cared to be around him. It was my reliance on God that prevented disaster from striking our home. Satan had again tried to destroy our family by his deceptions, but God had His own plan. One would think I would never doubt again.

Now, back to those grumbling, complaining Israelites. Numbers 14:1-4 tells us they would have rather returned to Egypt or died in the wilderness than go on. *"Then all the congregation lifted up their voices and cried, and the people wept that night. All the sons of Israel grumbled against Moses and Aaron; and the whole congregation said to them, 'Would that we had died in the land of Egypt! Or would that we had died in this wilderness! Why is the LORD bringing us into this land, to fall by the sword? Our wives and our little ones will become plunder; would it not be better for us to return to Egypt?' So, they said to one another, 'Let us appoint a leader and return to Egypt.'"* God forbid that we would ever get to the place that our circumstances would become so distressing that we would desire to return to Egypt…return to bondage, to surrender once again to the chains of sin, to the chains of despair. To say, "I have had enough, Lord. Trusting You is just too hard." Even after all the blessings, all the provision, and all the wonder that brought deliverance, to say, "I just can't take it anymore." That is what they were saying, and that is what we are saying when we give up, when we lose heart, when we lose hope, when we turn aside. Even knowing that He gave his son Jesus to be crucified for our salvation. We are saying, "I don't trust You. I don't believe

You…You lied." *God is not pleased with this lack of faith.* He loves us and is merciful, but there are consequences to our unbelief.

Do you want to know what God said to Israel concerning their unbelief? Read with me in Numbers 14:22-24: *"Surely all the men who have seen My glory and My signs which I performed in Egypt and in the wilderness, yet have put Me to the test these ten times and have not listened to My voice, shall by no means see the land which I swore to their fathers, nor shall any of those who spurned Me see it. But My servant Caleb, because he has had a different spirit and has followed Me fully, I will bring into the land which he entered, and his descendants shall take possession of it.* Then look down to verses 28-30: *"Say to them, 'As I live,' says the LORD, 'just as you have spoken in My hearing, so I will surely do to you; your corpses will fall in this wilderness, even all your numbered men, according to your complete number from twenty years old and upward, who have grumbled against Me. Surely you shall not come into the land in which I swore to settle you, except Caleb the son of Jephunneh and Joshua the son of Nun.'"* And that, my friend, is exactly what happened.

God cannot bring us into a promised land full of blessings when we walk in such unbelief, when we continue to complain and grumble against Him or, (in modern translation) when we talk about our lack, have pity parties, worry about paying the bills, fear our future, and sometimes even wish for death.

You may be saying that this story about the deliverance from Egypt all happened in the Old Testament, under the Old Covenant—a covenant of judgment—and that we live under the New Covenant—a covenant of grace. And I say, you are right! Amen and amen! But I tell you that until we trust Him, in full surrender to the wisdom and direction of the Holy Spirit, and live by faith, we will not enter the Promised Land of peace and provision. There is no number of miracles or wonders that will make us trust God if we don't first believe in who He is—if we don't have faith in who we are following. Our faith *is* strengthened as we see the evidence of promises fulfilled once we believe, but we *must* believe first. We must trust in what He said in His Word. Then we will walk by faith and not by sight. Walking by faith will allow us to face a challenge with the assurance of God's provision the instant it is presented, instead of mulling through weeks of anguish and mental debate.

Belief in **the pardon** (Jesus Christ's sacrifice for our sins) saves us—walking by faith in **the provision** (Christ abounding love, wisdom, and power poured out through the ministry of the Holy Spirit) sustains us and elevates us.

Remember the story of Lazarus and the rich man in Luke 16:22-31: *"One day the beggar died and was carried by the angels to Abraham's side. And the rich man also died and was buried. In Hades, where he was in torment, he looked up and saw Abraham from afar, with Lazarus by his side.*

"So, he cried out, 'Father Abraham, have mercy on me and send Lazarus to dip the tip of his finger in water and cool my tongue. For I am in agony in this fire.'

"But Abraham answered, 'Child, remember that during your lifetime you received your good things, while Lazarus received bad things. But now he is comforted here, while you are left to suffer. And besides all this, a great chasm has been fixed between us and you, so that even those who wish cannot cross from here to you, nor can anyone cross from there to us.'

"'Then I beg you, father,' he said, 'send Lazarus to my father's house, for I have five brothers. Let him warn them so they will not also end up in this place of torment.'

"But Abraham replied, 'They have Moses and the prophets; let your brothers listen to them.'

"'No, father Abraham,' he said, 'but if someone is sent to them from the dead, they will repent.'

"Then Abraham said to him, 'If they do not listen to Moses and the prophets, they will not be persuaded even if someone rises from the dead.'"

Our persuasion is only as great as our belief. No matter what we see, we must believe that God is who He says He is, that His Word is true, and His promises are true. We must believe without seeing a dead man rise, *but because our Savior rose!*

Consider this: We find ourselves in financial straits and ask God for help. God sees our distress and has Fed Ex deliver a box full of $100 bills right to the door. The label reads, "From Heaven." We rip the box open, finding a note that says, *"This is God. I thought you could use this."* We're ecstatic! Of course, we vow that we will never doubt again. I dare say, the next time things get tough, we might find ourselves reneging on that vow. The joy and excitement of the miraculous provision soon diminishes when the storm once again bears down. Remember the story of Jesus feeding the five thousand with the five loaves and two fishes? When everyone was satisfied, Jesus told the disciples to collect what was left. They gathered twelve baskets of leftovers. Immediately they got into their boats to cross to the other side. Jesus lay down in the boat to rest and went to sleep. Halfway out, a life-threatening squall came up, tossing the boat about on the swells as crashing waves broke over them. Fearing for their lives, they panicked, waking Jesus, asking how on earth he could sleep when they were about to lose their lives. Jesus strongly rebuked their lack of faith. You see what I mean? The disciples had just witnessed an unbelievable miracle—they had the leftovers to prove it—yet here they were. They had just received what equated to a big box of money from Fed Ex, and it didn't take a day for them to lose their faith for His provision in the storm. *They didn't really know who they were following.* You see, they *were* following Jesus, but they had yet to recognize who He was.

It might take a month or two for us, given how strong our faith is, but I suspect our faith would falter. I suspect something like that has happened to you. It has for me. An unexpected check in the mail, or someone slipped a $100 bill into your hand when you didn't know where your next meal was coming from. You might immediately praise God, and then scratch your head wondering how they knew. Do you think we have a hard time recognizing God? Maybe we do give Him the initial credit for the blessing but soon find a more practical reason why it happened. The box of money from Fed Ex—we start trying to figure out who might have sent it.

Today there may be no instant relief in sight, no immediate answer to your dilemma. There appears to be no way out, in the natural. Remember ladies, God can make a way when there seems to be no way. He proved it to the Israelites when He parted the Sea. He has proven it to us. We are not dealing with the natural, but with the supernatural. There is a way to see past your present circumstances, but it takes supernatural vision. We must look through the lens of hope and walk in the power, and the presence, and the provision of the One who created everything we see. Walk in the hope that something good is on the other side. He can calm our storm, just like he calmed it for the disciples. He can feed our families, just like He fed the five thousand. He can heal us, heal our children like He healed the leper. If we can hold on to the miracles we have already seen, the promises He has already fulfilled (the evidence,) we can walk in hope that He will do it again.

~~~~~~~~

September 11, 2001, our nation stood still, brought to its knees when the Twin Towers were brought down. When the heinous act of terrorism breached our borders, it breached our home. I lived in Austin at the time and remember walking into the bank that morning and the tellers running to greet me, to show me what was happening on the TV. I went to my office in a daze, unable to grasp what I had just seen, until the thought stabbed me like a knife—What would this mean for my son? It was an act of war, and he was a Marine. He was among the first deployed. In two days, he shipped out. It was weeks before we heard from him…months before he would return home. As the horror unfolded in the weeks following the initial attack, we grieved and prayed for our nation and prayed for our son. God's grace kept our nation, and God's grace kept us. When the anxieties of the unknown started to overwhelm, I asked my Father for peace and prayed once again for my son's protection. Offering up my petition, I recalled His Word that says, *"be anxious for nothing"*, and His mercy of peace surpassed all my understanding. In the stillness of the desert, I trusted my Father and rested in Him. I hoped in something good, and He brought it to pass—He brought Shawn home. Once again, God had proven His faithfulness. My son served during 9/11, like thousands of others, and God brought us through to the good on the other side.

John 14:27 *"Peace I leave with you, My peace I give to you; not as the world gives do I give to you. Let not your heart be troubled, neither let it be afraid."*

Philippians 4:6-7 *"Be anxious for nothing, but in everything by prayer and supplication, with thanksgiving, let your requests be made known to God; and the peace of God, which surpasses all understanding, will guard your hearts and minds through Christ Jesus."*

When tragedy hits, we must be ready. Do not deny yourself entrance into the Promised Land, the place of peace that surpasses natural understanding. Do not cry out to return to Egypt. Right there in the desert, when the enemy is bearing down, STAND! Remember the miracles of the past. Stand on the promise of the present. BELIEVE! Caleb believed for forty years. He remembered the miracles of the past and held on to the promise of God. He entered the Promised Land.

If I haven't convinced you yet, maybe this story will. Christmas morning, 2008, was a wonderful, joyous morning. All our grown sons were home, sitting around the tree tearing into presents, laughing, excited, drinking cocoa, when my husband noticed a lump on Frank Jr.'s neck. When asked what it was, Frank Jr. said it was a pulled muscle, and that he had another one under his arm. We panicked. Two days later, we learned he had Hodgkin's Lymphoma. He was twenty-two years old. Every good thing, every miracle we had ever witnessed or experienced, evaporated...*for a minute*. But soon we took our stand and went to war. I became a warrior for my son. I put my armor on and picked up my sword.

Sitting across from the admissions nurse, I watched my young beautiful son fill out a DNR (Do Not Resuscitate) form. He looked up and looked at me with such longing—understanding the finality of what he had just done. He folded it and handed it to me. I quietly tucked it into my purse. A constant reminder of his fragile life...I would carry the Do Not Resuscitate form with me for a year.

Frank Sr. was singing with *Legacy Five* at the time, and once again, we had thousands of people across the globe go to their knees and go to God on our behalf. Every day we received hundreds of emails with encouraging messages from people committed to prayer on our behalf. Cards, letters, candy, and blankets poured in, building our faith, building Frank Jr.'s faith. Frank even received calls from Dr. David Jeremiah, who was a friend of *Legacy Five* and had fought and won a battle with Hodgkin's years earlier. He, too, was standing with us in our battle.

We didn't get an immediate miracle like we did with Jason's healing from the brain tumor. It was a long, hard-fought battle with many highs and lows. I remember halfway through the treatment, we *thought* we had the miracle. The doctor brought us in and showed us the PET scan: no tumors, no cancer! We were overwhelmed with relief and gratitude. Well, we took the before and after PET scans, and Frank Jr. and I headed to Opryland with Frank to the *Legacy Five* Memorial Day Celebration to celebrate with L5 and a few thousand friends who had stood with us. As it turned out, Mike Huckabee and his sweet wife Janet were there as part of his book tour, which added an extra blessing to the celebration. We got to share our joy and excitement with them. What a treat! Pictures and all! Now for those of you who don't know me, I am a political wannabe. I have never served in office but have aspired to work in the White House for as long as I can remember. The Lord even dropped a little phrase into my spirit in 2004—*Political Missionary*—and I am still waiting for it to come to pass. So, celebrating my son's healing with Janet Huckabee was priceless. She will never know what that quiet conversation on her bus meant to me. Well, maybe she will.

Now imagine, after such a high, to get the news: The cancer is back and is back with a vengeance. Just a month after celebrating, believing God had delivered us, the aggressive cancer mutated and became immune to the chemo. The tumors had grown during the last treatment cycle. Frank Jr.'s chance of survival plummeted to thirty percent. We were confronted with the reality that we might lose our youngest son. The possibility that he wasn't going to make it was real. We were shaken...*for a minute.*

Immediately, Frank Jr.'s oncologist referred us to an expert in stem cell transplants, and a new level of faith was needed. We were tested beyond measure. Now, you might question at this point, "Where was God?" We did...*for a minute.*

Listen. It's easy even for non-Christians to live in peace if everything they ever wanted or desired was given to them. If they had perfect mates, all the money they ever needed; strong, healthy children; and healthy bodies, even non-Christians may find some contentment. But it's *how we respond in the struggle*— —in times of lack, in the fiery furnace of life, the times when we are backed against the Red Sea—that sets us apart. It's in the fiery trial, in the darkest night, that our light of faith shines the brightest, showing others the way. It's when our hope in Christ moves us forward, with high expectations of something good being on the other side, that we can move others forward.

We can't hope for something we already have, but we hope for those things we don't have. Romans 8:23-25 says, *"Not only that, but we also who have the first fruits of the Spirit, even we ourselves groan within ourselves, eagerly waiting for the adoption, the redemption of our body. For we were saved in this hope, but hope that is seen is not hope; for why does one still hope for what he sees? But if we hope for what we do not see, we eagerly wait for it with perseverance."* If your present circumstances are wrought with despair and confusion, maybe even death, I believe God would challenge you to lift it all to Him and begin to hope for a new day—a day of deliverance—a day of peace. Then trust Him to bring it about. Trust in His Word. Put on the full armor and make your stand. Watch for His blessings to be manifested, and they will be. Expect Him to move on your behalf, and He will. You'll enter a new land…a land flowing with milk and honey. You will taste the sweetness of His mercy and peace. Go ahead and smile. It feels good to simply have hope—hope in the good that is just on the other side—the other side of the circumstance or the other side of heaven, either is good.

The day before we checked into Medical City Hospital to start the process of a stem cell transplant, Frank Jr. and I sat at a local restaurant having a "last meal," if you will, when he looked at me and asked me a question that took my breath...*for a minute.* "Mom, how can you go to work every day when I am dying with cancer?" He never knew the searing of my soul at that moment.

I answered as calmly as if he had asked what I wanted for dinner: "It is my job that provides the insurance that allows me to take such good care of you, so we don't have to worry about that. I have to do my part."

"Okay, Mom. I understand. Thank you for taking such good care of me," he responded. And that was that.

The months of high-dose chemo ravaged my son to the point of death. Seeing the deterioration of his body was more than I could bear. We almost lost him instantly on two occasions. Once, when Frank was rinsing dishes in the small kitchen on the twelfth floor, he heard Frank Jr. scream his name. He told me he could hardly breathe as he bolted to Frank Jr.'s room. It was like a nightmare. Frank Jr. was bathed in blood. The line to his port had become disconnected, and blood was flowing like an open faucet. How do you recover from such an image? From such an experience? GOD.

The second time, once again Frank was with him. I was at work. It was the day of the transplant. Within seconds after inserting the syringe filled with his stem cells, he went into cardiac arrest. He was allergic to the liquid nitrogen they had been stored in. But God heard Frank's prayer, and once again, God brought him through. Frank Jr.'s battle with cancer robbed him of many things, but it didn't take his faith, and it didn't take his life.

My son, Frank Jr., celebrated ten years of being cancer free August 19, 2019.

"You will keep him in perfect peace, whose mind is stayed on You, because he trusts in You." Isaiah 26:3

Chapter Four – Die to Self, or Self-Destruct

Dying to self, or self-denial, has been preached to us our whole Christian lives. Women especially (yes, I did say that,) understand sacrificial living. In general, putting the needs of our families before tending to our own personal needs comes naturally and tends to be expected. We know what I am saying is true. Just as we sit down with our morning coffee, the phone rings. Our husband forgot his briefcase and asks, if we're not terribly busy, would we mind bringing it to him? On our way out the door, we notice our son's lunch box sitting on the counter and grab it, knowing the school is three miles in the opposite direction. Or we have a big presentation at work, and a new suit would give us just the confidence we need, but instead of buying ourselves a new suit, we buy one for our son so he can take his date to homecoming looking his best…and so it goes. However, dying to self means far more than denying ourselves of trivial material things or pleasures. It means denying *self-will*. We see in Romans 12:1-2 that surrendering our bodies as sacrifices is merely our "acceptable service."

> *"Therefore, I urge you, brethren, by the mercies of God, to present your bodies a living and holy sacrifice, acceptable to*

God, which is your spiritual service of worship. And do not be conformed to this world, but be transformed by the renewing of your mind, so that you may prove what the will of God is, that which is good and acceptable and perfect."

It is simply our reasonable service to God, because of the high price He paid, to live our lives surrendered to His will.

Colossians 3:2-3 says, *"Set your mind on the things above, not on the things that are on earth. For you have died and your life is hidden with Christ in God."*

When we accepted Christ, we acknowledged He bought our salvation with the shedding of His blood.

1 Peter 1:18-19 makes it clear: *"knowing that you were not redeemed with corruptible things, like silver or gold, from your aimless conduct received by tradition from your fathers, but with the precious blood of Christ, as of a lamb without blemish and without spot."*

Our bodies, our wills, our desires, are no longer ours, but His; hence, dying to self is just what it says. We die so Christ can live out His life through us. We can't rise and climb out of the coffin.

Again, in 1 Peter 4:1-2, we see this reiterated. *"Therefore, since Christ suffered for us in the flesh, arm yourselves also with the same mind, for he who has suffered in the flesh has ceased from sin, that he no longer should live the rest of his time in the flesh for the lusts of men, but for the will of God."*

God's will is for all to be saved, and for His children to have abundant, joy-filled lives set apart for His service.

*"The thief does not come except to steal, and to kill, and to destroy. I have come that they may have life, and that they may have **it** more abundantly" John 10:10*

The "**it**" factor, in John 10:10, as my husband has preached about on many Sunday mornings, is not the "it" factor the secular world refers to when referring to a charismatic individual. **It** is the charismatic presence and power of the Holy Spirit *in* an individual.

As I stated earlier in the book, Paul himself made this statement, *"For to me, to live is Christ, and to die is gain. But if I live on in the flesh, this will mean fruit from my labor; yet what I shall choose I cannot tell. For I am hard-pressed between the two, having a desire to depart and be with Christ, which is far better. Nevertheless, to remain in the flesh is more needful for you. And being confident of this, I know that I shall remain and continue with you all for your progress and joy of faith, that your rejoicing for me may be more abundant in Jesus Christ by my coming to you again."*

I expect by now you are tired of me preaching. Hold on. It's for our good. The sooner we die, the sooner we burst through the grave of sin and doubt and despair and spring to new life—a Spirit-led life lived for the sake of others, a life free from the cares of this world because we live for the One who holds the world in His hand. Does a corpse have a care in the world? No. Have you ever seen a corpse going to a psychiatrist? No. Dying to self doesn't mean death in the way our finite minds understand it. It means life and life more abundantly.

But if we walk in the flesh, the problems of this world will bury us. It's easy, with all life's demands, to get caught up in negative thoughts. We begin to focus on how much we're giving out and how little we're getting back. It's easy to lose sight of our purpose when all we see are mounds of laundry. We could give way to the notion that this Christian life is one of utter sacrifice without joy or reward until we get to heaven. Satan ratchets us down slowly until we acquiesce, becoming resigned to a lower state of living, believing this is all there is for now. Before we know it, we're dwelling on all the negative aspects of our lives and forgetting the good. The negative thoughts snowball into despair, or maybe even depression, leaving us stymied… silent…and still. Or, worse than that, Satan ratchets us up to rebellion, and those negative thoughts produce negative words and actions that become weapons in his hands.

I'm not implying that our lives will be wrought with heartache from dawn' til dusk. What I'm trying to get us to see is that if we will die to self and surrender our wills on the altar of sacrifice, we can live abundant lives. God's Word declares it so. We must die before we can live. We cannot *pretend* to die to self, walking around like zombies. Our flesh will decay. The *pretense* of sacrificial living will literally put you in the grave. But, being resurrected in the likeness and image of Christ, doing good works through the power of His Spirit, will bring the abundant life. God has the power to bring life from death, and He has put that power in us. If we set our minds on pursuing our wills, it will destroy us; it will separate us from the Holy Spirit. If we set our minds on pursuing God's will, He will direct us through this chaotic world, guarding our hearts and minds along the path He has destined for us.

We may think it's impossible to live this kind of life, but stop and consider the finality of death as you walk by a coffin with the corpse utterly still, void of life and spirit, unable to think, move or speak…no will of its own. The person is dead, and it is not possible for them to get up from the coffin and live again. Their flesh is dead; their spirit is gone; they have no self-will. When we say we die to self, it should hold the same finality as the physical death I just illustrated. How, then, could we lift a finger or say a word unless there is a new spirit in us? And if there is a new spirit, then there is a new will. This new spirit is the Spirit of God, and this new will is the will of God. The old spirit is no more. The old ways are no longer evident, but now we move, speak, and have our being through Jesus Christ. Even the slightest gesture is no longer possible for one who is dead––a wink of the eye, a tilt of the head, implying a lustful desire––these are gone…or *should be*.

Heaven forbid we find ourselves in some unlikely situation during one of those nights we're alone, wondering what has gone wrong in our marriage, or, after years of being single, wondering if God is ever going to show up—and rise up out of the coffin, becoming the epitome of the *walking dead*. The initial stage seems innocent enough. There's no harm in wanting to be appreciated…wanting to be noticed…wanting a little companionship—but with Satan's influence, this innocent little desire could easily lead to something that is not so innocent. It could lead to a flirtatious gesture toward someone we may not even know. Rest assured, when that happens, we are in the danger zone. RUN! Flee the very appearance of evil.

Now, I'm not presuming you will fall into this trap, and I'm not being condemning if you have fallen, but if so, it needs to be fixed. I understand the feelings, emotions, and desires of women who all too often get overlooked in the daily affairs of the ministry, or in their marriage, or in life in general, and know that the possibility is there. If you are living on the brink, if your marriage is in jeopardy, there may need to be some spiritual, psychological, or relational counseling. Reach for Christ and reach out to someone for help. Do not be duped by Satan. Do not listen to his lies and start feeling sorry for yourself. It's a trap! I hear it now, "My husband should love me like Christ loved the church." He should! But ladies, we do not live in a perfect world, and our husbands are not perfect. They are *being* perfected every day like we are, so don't have expectations they cannot meet, or you and they will be sorely disappointed. No one can live under that kind of pressure. Something or someone will have to give, or the lid is going to blow. Your marriage could explode. Release the pressure. Lower your expectations a little and pray for him.

The good news? If we allow Christ to live His life through us, denying our self-will, we can be freed from the seduction. We can be freed from the chains of self-interest, no longer held captive to the lusts of the flesh. Oh, there will always be temptations. Satan will see to that, but our hearts and minds will be guarded. We will see it coming, and with the shield of faith, we can stop the fiery darts before they penetrate our heart.

As I mentioned earlier, Philippians 4:6-7 says, *"Be anxious for nothing, but in everything by prayer and supplication, with thanksgiving, let your requests be made known to God; and the peace of God, which surpasses all understanding, will guard your hearts and minds through Christ Jesus."*

So, let go of self, lay back down in the coffin, and allow God to resurrect you into new life. There is no greater liberty than total trust in God and total abandonment to self.

This story may shock you a little, but I would be remiss if I didn't share about the first time I lay back down in the coffin and allowed God to resurrect me.

Two years after my divorce, my life was starting to normalize somewhat. I was in school and working and taking care of my two sons. I had a good church family and a group of friends who loved me, when one day I got a phone call. My ex-sister-in-law broke the news that my ex-husband had been charged with murder. During a violent encounter, a woman had died. He wanted me to come and testify on his behalf. My first thought was, *That could have been me,* but I heard her out. While in jail, he had surrendered his life to Christ and was asking for my help. I prayed and told the Lord if it was what He wanted I would do it. I didn't tell anyone about the phone call. I knew what they would say: *"Are you crazy? Of course, you can't go."* I wanted to hear from God. He spoke. I called her and relayed that I was willing to come but that I could not lie for him. If they asked about adultery, if they asked about abuse, I could not lie. He agreed. A few days later, I was on a plane. He was now out on bail, and his attorney had arranged for the three of us to talk. The attorney's conclusion? I would not be a good witness during the trial, but if I was willing to reconcile with him if he got probation, I could be a valuable witness during the sentencing phase. Once again, I prayed and told the Lord I would do it if that is what He wanted. I would reconcile if he got probation…but if he didn't, I would be free to move forward, free from the condemnation of divorce, free to remarry. I prayed all night. I didn't want to hurt him with my testimony; I only wanted to do good. The courtroom scene was like a scene from the latest thriller. The prosecutor was running for District Attorney, and the media was in full force. His older brother (someone you wouldn't want to mess with) was my bodyguard and escort in and out of the courtroom, shielding my face with a newspaper. (I told you it was like a movie.)

My ex-husband was convicted of first-degree murder. Now it was my turn to make a stand for God…to die to self…to lay down all my fears. I was called to the witness stand. My heart stopped. My next breath was God's breath. My words would be His words. The prosecutor was kind. He had only one question for me: "Will you reconcile with him if he is given probation?" I stopped shaking and looked him in the eyes. *"Yes,"* I responded.

He smiled and said, *"Thank you. You can step down now."*

My ex-husband was sentenced to forty years. I took the boys to visit him several times before his early release, eight years later.

When I tell you that we must die to self, I know what I am talking about. No one saw **me** on the stand that day in the courtroom…they saw Christ. I had died. He was living His life through me.

We may very well have just cause to say, "Hold on a minute; something is wrong with this picture." That's okay. When things are off balance, they need to be made right. We need to operate in the order and structure that God ordained for our marriages and for our lives. However, there is a right way to address it. We must know when to open our mouths and when to keep them closed. And the only way to know is to walk in His Spirit. Pray before uttering a single word. We must consider our motives. Are they for our good or for the good of all? Are we concerned with our husbands' souls? With their relationships with God? With their ministries? Remember, if he has a right relationship with God, he will have a right relationship with you. Are we concerned with our friend's broken heart, or ours? We have no ability to change a person, but God does. It is not God's will that we live in a constant state of abuse or neglect, or sadness, or discontent. His word says that *"He who did not spare His own Son, but delivered Him up for us all, how shall He not with Him also freely give us all things?"* With the intervention of the Holy Spirit and the intercession of Jesus Christ through prayer, lives and people can be changed. We are not the change agent. We must set our hearts and minds on the Holy Spirit and allow God to bring about change…allow God to give those things into our hands that He desires us to have.

Romans 8:5-6 says, *"For those who live according to the flesh set their minds on the things of the flesh, but those who live according to the Spirit, the things of the Spirit. For to be carnally minded is death, but to be spiritually minded is life and peace."*

Let go of any destructive thoughts. Don't be tormented any longer. Die to your own will. Die to self that you might live an abundant life in Christ. I admit it is easier said than done, but *I have done it* and continue to do it daily. It is a daily act of faith and trust and surrender. ***But…there is rest in surrender.***

We must live for the sake of others. We must live for those who will be touched by our lives—touched by our witnesses, our smiles, our joy, by the words of truth we speak—and by the strength they see through our perseverance. Be a witness to a life lived in Christ—a life of power and beauty and peace. *Our purpose is greater than our human emotions.*

Think about this: From the very moment that Jesus came to understand the Father's will, He understood that His reason for living was to die. His Father had given Him up to be a sacrifice for all of mankind so that man could be reconciled back to Him. His sole purpose in life was to die.

What if Jesus had said that His Father had asked too much of Him? Where would we be? How little our troubles seem when compared to the sacrifice Jesus made. Don't be perplexed and distraught when you encounter trials. This is the way of the Christian. Satan *is* trying to kill us, you know. The Word says we will be met with opposition but that we should consider it joy.

James 1:2-4: *"My brethren, count it all joy when you fall into various trials, knowing that the testing of your faith produces patience. But let patience have its perfect work, that you may be perfect and complete, lacking nothing."*

What a wonderful thought: to be lacking in nothing! We will lack nothing if we pass the tests of faith…if we endure.

Let me share one of the most gut-wrenching times of my life—a time that tested me beyond limits—a time that tested my resolve to be a witness. It tested the very nature of who I am in Christ…a test I almost failed. In March of 2000, I got a call from my mom telling me that my dad had been in a tragic accident. I flew to California that day, only to learn that he would never recover. I would never be able to speak to him again. I would never be able to tell him how much I loved him again. His brain stem had been severed. After a week of being on life support, the decision had to be made to remove it. I wanted him freed to go to heaven. My mom wanted him to remain. She needed his check to survive. I'm not diminishing my Mom; she was afraid. What I didn't know at the time was that my dad would have to die within one year of the accident for my mom to get the insurance money. Ten months later, I had to have surgery on my spine, and I asked my mom to remove my dad from life support so I could attend his funeral before my surgery. I wanted Frank to sing "*His Eye is on the Sparrow.*" I wanted to say goodbye. By that time, I had learned about the time limit for his death to be attributed to the accident, and I knew she would want the insurance money. I didn't hear from her, yet I had to go ahead with the surgery. Three days later, lying in a recliner with a brace on, my sister called to tell me that my dad was buried that day and that my mom's boyfriend had carried his coffin. Anger consumed me. Rage exploded in my mind and heart. My pain was unbearable. My ache for my dad, and my hate for my mom, buried me. I could not be consoled. Frank tried, but nothing could comfort me. Then, somehow the Holy Spirit broke through. I *had* to forgive if I was going to go on. My freedom would come *only* through forgiving her. Her freedom would come only through my forgiveness. Three weeks of pure hate had almost killed me, but one second of surrender gave me life. I did forgive and spent the next seven years loving and caring for my mom, even after she called one day to tell me that my dad who had died *was not really my father.*

Once again, my mom's fear had defeated her. She didn't consider what that revelation would do to me. Instead, she wanted me to find my real father for *her* sake. She was sick and scared of being alone, and she wanted him to take care of her. I searched for him. When I finally discovered who he was, I learned that he had died one month earlier. I was not disappointed. He had never been my father. But I did feel sorry for my mom, whom I encouraged until her passing in 2008. I showed her the love and forgiveness of Christ so she could find forgiveness. I planted the seed for *her* to have new life. That's when I learned: **The path for planting is formed in the burden of the plowing.** Accepting and understanding my mom's fears formed the path; Forgiving her for her actions driven by those fears was the seed. The harvest—her soul.

No matter how hard the burden, look toward the harvest and put your hand on the plow.

"I have been crucified with Christ; it is no longer I who live, but Christ lives in me; and the life which I now live in the flesh I live by faith in the Son of God, who loved me and gave Himself for me." Galatians 2:20

Chapter Five – LIVING ABOVE THE CIRCUMSTANCES

Why do we allow life to turn us into someone we are not? Someone we don't want to be—someone we don't even like? We drift from our own nature, the nature of Christ, into someone we don't recognize in the mirror. Anger and grief make us quick to snap, and ugly hateful thoughts war in our mind. We fixate on our circumstances, or a dilemma, or a tragedy, for so long, it literally becomes our idol—being alone, serving in the shadows; the fifty pounds we can't lose; the constant pain from arthritis; the death of a parent; the death of a spouse; the infidelity of a husband; the disloyalty of a trusted friend; a child deep in sin and addiction; a child with cancer; a son serving on foreign soil in the throes of war. We become so consumed with IT that we lose ourselves in our pain. *It is understandable.* But hear me: *Anything that draws our attention away from God is the wrong thing.* Oh, we are going to mourn, we are going to get angry, we are going to grieve, and, I dare say, we are going to hate, but if you *stay* there, it's wrong. Pain is real. Sorrow is real. Hurt is real. Anger is real, but...*we can't stay there.* My pain and anger did not lift me to the heavens. It took me to the deepest pit, and it will take you there as well. Our Father does not set us up to fail. He sees it all.

He knows how much is too much. Trust me, just when we think it is too much, He surprises us with a way of escape. He wants us to trust in His eternal love and sovereignty. He wants us to trust Him even when we don't understand…especially when we don't understand.

Paul expressed it well. *2 Corinthians 4:8-18 says, "We are hard-pressed on every side, yet not crushed; we are perplexed, but not in despair; persecuted, but not forsaken; struck down, but not destroyed—always carrying about in the body the dying of the Lord Jesus, that the life of Jesus also may be manifested in our body. For we who live are always delivered to death for Jesus' sake, that the life of Jesus also may be manifested in our mortal flesh. So, then death is working in us, but life in you.*

"And since we have the same spirit of faith, according to what is written, 'I believed and therefore I spoke.' we also believe and therefore speak, knowing that He who raised up the Lord Jesus will also raise us up with Jesus, and will present us with you. For all things are for your sakes, that grace, having spread through the many, may cause thanksgiving to abound to the glory of God. Therefore, we do not lose heart. Even though our outward man is perishing, yet the inward man is being renewed day by day. For our light affliction, which is but for a moment, is working for us a far more exceeding and eternal

weight of glory, while we do not look at the things which are seen, but at the things which are not seen. For the things which are seen are temporary, but the things which are not seen are eternal."

What happened to living out what Paul professed in 2 Corinthians 4? How could he call it *"light"* affliction? Well, consider his next statement: *"which is but for a moment."* The formula for living it out, the reason we can call it light affliction, is because *it is temporary*. Blink and this life will be over. The formula for living above the circumstances of this life, living above every difficulty we will face, is simply taking hold of the eternal and letting go of the temporal. Looking at the big picture. Looking to our big God and seeing our circumstances from His perspective. How do we accomplish this? We *don't*, at least not in our own power. It only comes from walking day by day, minute by minute, in the power of the Holy Spirit.

I must admit that if it had not been for the sovereign work that God did in me before Frank went into the ministry, I'm not so sure I could have survived my role as a minister's wife. Remember the story I told you earlier, when I found myself on the floor scraping up that donkey dung? I was in the shadows. No one could see what I was doing. No one knew the motives of my heart. But God knew. My act of yielding and obeying did not go unnoticed by Him…not that I had any good thing in me that motivated me to do such an act; it was God who moved me to humility. As I cleaned up that mess, God saw my heart. God chose me, acknowledged me, and called me. His seal of validation was seared on my heart. I needed no other.

Can you imagine the God of all creation acknowledging you and calling you by name? Remember Hagar, Sarah's maidservant who was met by the angel of the Lord when fleeing Sarah's presence?

"Then she called the name of the LORD who spoke to her, You-Are-the-God-Who-Sees; for she said, 'Have I also here seen Him who sees me?'" Genesis 16:13.

She was awed by knowing that God saw her in her distress and promised her protection and provision. But she had to return to Sarah…she had to submit to her place of serving.

Hearing God call our names is a call I believe we all hunger to hear. My words are not enough to express how His words changed me. The words He spoke that night still resonate deep in my soul.

"Libby, this is what you will have to do for me. You will be in the shadows cleaning up the mess. You will have to do the hard part, the part no one will see."

That calling is what carried me through my anguish and sorrow. When I lay on my bed crying, His words stayed with me through the night. He reminded me of how grateful I had been when I heard Him call my name, when He chose me out of the sea of people to be of service to Him. I remembered saying, "Thank you for choosing me. Thank you for seeing me. Thank you for giving me a work to do, for calling me out." As I recalled that night, that moment I heard His voice, all the heartfelt emotions would once again stir me and strengthen me, moving me forward, renewing my joy in fulfilling my purpose.

I believe my purpose is to invite you to get on the floor with me and scoop up some "donkey dung," allowing it to become your experience—your calling to surrender to whatever God has for you to do. I believe the words He gave me that night were for you, also. Listen, and you will hear your name. He has called us into a place of service, a hard place, a hard work…just like Paul. And just like Paul, He sees each one of you, counting you faithful for service. He has equipped us for it, whether it means being in the shadows or in the spotlight. Perhaps there will be no applause, no recognition, no pats on the back, but that is of no consequence when we hear the voice of God asking us to do something. God sees and knows what is done in secret, and He will reward us. I know that to be true. Trust in that and rejoice in your calling. Be grateful for it. We must understand the importance of our roles. The ministry could not go on without those roles. Perhaps a lost soul watching us could not go on without them. The clamor of self will is hard to push down if we don't get this. I know it is a hard place to be, but if we can hold onto the faithfulness of God and simply trust in Him, we will honor Him through our service. If we truly trust in someone, we rely on them, have faith in them, and put our confidence in them. To trust means complete surrender, being vulnerable to the one we trust in. But know this; putting our trust in the right someone—in the Lord Jesus Christ—establishes safety, security, confidence, loyalty, certainty, and stability for our lives.

God is love and His love never fails. He is always the same: unchanging, forever faithful. If we put our trust in Him, we will never be disappointed. Do not doubt. If we trust in Him, He will give us the desires of our hearts.

Learning to live above the circumstances, to live behind the scenes, or to live in the spotlight comes from trusting God enough to let go of the temporary and take hold of the eternal. Whether abhorred for our deformities or obsessively adored for our beauty, we must let go of this temporary station in life and know we are all royal daughters of the King who created it all. We must look through the lens of eternity, seeing the prize that's before us. As we rise above the circumstances, pressing on toward the eternal goal, storing up treasured souls for His Kingdom, we will soar on the wings of eagles. His Word says it, and I tell you it is true. I have ridden the wings.

Walking by faith in an everlasting God and not by mortal sight becomes as natural as an eagle flying. Through the power of the Holy Spirit that abides in us, our vision reaches far beyond our natural sight. We see the big picture. We see all that God intends for us to have. We are lifted to the heavenlies—His Throne Room, His majesty, the streets of gold, and the mansion He has prepared for us. But more than that, we see the smile of our Father. Jesus said that we are in Him, and He is in us. If that is so, then a part of us is already in heaven. A part of us is seated with Him at the right hand of the Father. When I need to be encouraged, I go to where He is. I look around heaven for a while and rest there with Him. Lifted out of the turmoil and anxieties that confound me, separated from the hurts of this world, I enjoy my eternal home. Refreshed with an eternal perspective, once again I am made aware of my purpose—the purpose of lighting the way for others to get to Him. My pain and sorrow diminish in the light of this new awareness. Having an eternal perspective and taking hold of the revelation and reality of who we are and what we have in Christ will change us like it changed Paul. *"For our light affliction, which is but for a moment, is working for us a far more exceeding and eternal weight of glory."* He knew that the One who raised Jesus will also raise us. His desire was for all to be raised with Jesus, and so his suffering was worth it all. The truth set him free, and the truth will set us free. We shouldn't be spending all our time looking for a way of escape; *we should be the way of escape*. Our light should shine brightly, illuminating the path for others to find their way out…to find their way to Him.

The Word says we can bring every thought captive. I simply say "no" to the bad thoughts and "yes" to that which is good for my edification. It's a discipline that is only accomplished by making a marked decision to follow God's instructions to dwell on that which is good. Our ability to dwell with Jesus today, right now, is within our own hearts. Don't suffer under the weight of these temporary surroundings; live the eternal life now. The day we accepted Christ as our Savior, the day we were "born again," was the day we were adopted by the Father. From that point in time, we were made joint heirs with Christ…daughters of the Most High God. That day we were granted access to all that is His. The vault of heaven stands open. Reach in and get a handful—a handful of peace, a handful of joy, a handful of worth, a handful of love.

But if we are going to get "handfuls," our hands must be empty. We must empty out the guilt, the pain, the grief, the anger. We must let go of all the destructive lies we are holding on to. Letting go is our victory. Letting go will utterly defeat the enemy.

Remember the children of Israel? They knew God had told them He was taking them to Canaan, the *"land flowing with milk and honey."* He told them He would give their enemies into their hands...but their hands were full of distrust, doubt, and fear, so they were not free to take hold of that promise. We know that we have the promise of eternity with God, that this life is but a vapor. All His eternal promises are right there for the taking. Learn from their mistake. Empty your hands and reach in.

I'm not making light of today's afflictions or implying that our trials are trite and insignificant, that they don't hurt, but we can't let the trials block our access to deliverance. We can't hold on to the pain that prevents us from holding on to the Deliverer. We can't let our desires keep Him from fulfilling His.

A woman's heart was designed with a longing to love and to nurture. Our emotions and desires were designed for good purposes, but when corrupted by Satan, we might find that our desires are left unsatisfied. When we become dissatisfied, we may move away from our husbands—from our marriages. We think the grass is greener on the other side, so we stray in search of something better. When we become dissatisfied, we may move away from God. We think there is more, and He is keeping it from us. Remember Eve. She thought there was more, and God was keeping it from her. Look where that got us.

Let's consider the prodigal son for a minute. Most say it was his sin that separated him from his father—and it was, but the drifting away started long before the sin of leaving. It started with a lack of love for his father or *a belief that he was not loved by his father*. It started with dissatisfaction. He was not satisfied; otherwise, he would not have desired to leave. If we are fully satisfied, we do not leave that which satisfies us. He knew his father, but he *did not **know** his father*. He did not know all that his father owned was already his, so he settled for less, and his "less" soon ran out. He demanded what was his today, forfeiting what was his in the future. He forfeited the one who could fully satisfy in exchange for Satan's temporary, counterfeit satisfaction. Like the NOW generation, the prodigal son's story was about being dissatisfied and wanting more and wanting it now…wanting what was owed to him. He thought his father was standing in the way of him living life to the fullest. He grabbed hold of the wrong thing and moved away from him.

In grave distress, the prodigal son eventually returned to his father and was overwhelmingly embraced with his love. Everything he had believed that caused him to move away was disproved that day, the day he went home was the day he experienced his father's love.

We must let go of the deceptions that Satan has infiltrated our minds with since we were small, the things that dictate self-focus and demand self-will, and the things that prevent total surrender to God. In today's culture, we must fight for the very right to surrender. Surrendering to a loving Father brings victory. Jesus understood that. He cried for the cup of sacrifice to be taken but surrendered to the will of His Father. He was beaten and bloodied and hung on a cross—*now, all things are subject to Him*. He has never asked us to hang on a cross or *maybe He has*.

"Then Jesus said to His disciples, 'If anyone desires to come after Me, let him deny himself, and take up his cross, and follow Me.'" Matthew 16:24

It is our choice to live in despair, nurturing our pain and misfortune, or to take hold of the promises of God and live in peace. No matter what our circumstances might be, God has made provision through His Holy Spirit to enable us to let go of the temporal and take hold of the eternal. He has enabled us to let go of the burden that is crushing us and pick up His burden, which is light. He has enabled us to die to self on the cross of surrender, so we can be lifted up.

Let me tell you a story. My friend's son, Steve, had a severe car accident as a teenager that left him a paraplegic. Once a strong, healthy boy, he became confined to a wheelchair. His mother told me that, as she was ironing one day and having a conversation with God, she asked Him to look at Steve's scarred and blistered hands from pushing the wheelchair, to look at how swollen and torn his flesh was. She cried out for Him to heal Steve's hands. "Look at his hands, Father. Please look at his hands." As she was interceding for Steve, God spoke to her and said, *"Have you looked at my Son's hands?"*

At that moment, she realized that her grief had blinded her. Not that a mother wouldn't grieve. Of course, we would. He expects that. But ***grief that becomes our sole focus is grief that destroys***, and God knows that. ***Grief that blinds us to God's love KILLS.*** Holding onto grief keeps us from holding onto God. ***We can't take hold of the only hand that can lead us through such horror, the only hand that can lead us through the valley of the shadow of death, to the green pastures, to the still waters, if our hands are holding onto something else.***

I don't know how many times she prayed for Steve and hoped for his healing. But when that hope wasn't realized, her faith diminished, and her vision blurred. She lost sight of God's sovereignty; she lost the ability to see any good *except for Steve's healing*. Her hope was no longer in Christ alone; her hope was in Steve alone. Her hope could not say, *"Not my will, but Your will."* Hoping for her son to be healed wasn't wrong. It was natural. I have hoped for my sons' healings, but hope in a singular outcome, not allowing for God's will, can plummet us into despair if the one thing we hope for isn't realized. Having hope that someone will be healed, when then they are not, has caused some to walk away from God.

Christ desired not to have to go to the cross, not to have to take on man's sin and be separated from His Father. He hoped for a different outcome when He asked the Father to take the cup from Him, but He surrendered His will to the will of the Father. If He hadn't relinquished His desire, *where would we be?*

If we hope for an end to the suffering and the suffering doesn't end, what do we do? When we've waited on God—year after year enduring the pain—with the expectation that it will end soon…and it doesn't? What do we do? We might find ourselves questioning God's love. We might find ourselves questioning His very existence. We might find ourselves building a golden calf of grief. That is what Satan would tell us to do.

Our only hope should be in Christ, who does not disappoint. We might not see the thing we hope for this side of heaven, or we might. Either way, our hope is realized.

The simple words, *"Have you looked at my Son's hands?"* spoke to Steve's mother so deeply that she was able to consider the pain God must have experienced as He watched His Son have nails driven into His hands, as He was nailed to a cross—a cross of humiliation that separated Him from His Son, as He asked Him to die for the sins of man. My friend and her son, Steve, had suffered greatly, but neither had been asked to suffer unto death. Neither had been separated from the love of each other or from the love of their Father. She was the one who had separated herself from the Father. She had become dissatisfied with what He had asked of her, with her lot in life. She no longer believed in His love for her or His love for her son. But the revelation that day of God's great love set her free. She remembered who He was. She remembered who she was. What had been hidden from view for years was in plain sight. She returned to the Father, and the Father embraced her with love.

She was now ready to defend Christ when confronted with *the* question: "How can a loving God let this happen to Steve?" You see, a person with a testimony is never at the mercy of someone with an argument. When the world screams that God isn't real, people with an experience still professing His love and mercy, prove He is.

Although we do have grave affliction and opposition on every side, it is not to the point of death…or, even if it was, we live and have life in Christ alone.

"And the Lord said, 'Simon, Simon! Indeed, Satan has asked for you, that he may sift you as wheat. But I have prayed for you, that your faith should not fail; and when you have returned to Me, strengthen your brethren.'" Luke 22:31-32

Chapter Six — Codependent on Christ

The feminist worldview that heralds, "Be independent. Submit to no one" has been inserting itself into our culture for some time now. Molding the next generation into the "Me" generation has been going on since the 1970s.

The "Me" generation in the United States is a term referring to the baby boomer generation and the self-involved qualities that some people associated with it. The baby boomers (Americans born during the 1946 to 1964 baby boom) were dubbed the "Me" generation by writer Tom Wolfe during the 1970s; Christopher Lasch was another writer who commented on the rise of a culture of narcissism among the younger generation. The phrase caught on with the general public, at a time when "self-realization" and "self-fulfillment" were becoming cultural aspirations to which young people supposedly ascribed higher importance than social responsibility. (4)

We see today that it starts in our elementary schools, where having high self-esteem is promoted by awarding every child a trophy, when only one child excelled, and it continues until they walk across the platform of our liberal college campuses, declaring their individualism as women. It's this distorted worldview indoctrination that eventually diminishes the need for God. "We can do all things within ourselves." That's what we're told. It's all about us. The danger, of course, is in not recognizing that the good in any of us is from God; that our abilities are gifts from God. Boldness, strength, confidence are all good things if you keep that in mind; after all, we didn't create ourselves. The Creator had something to do with it. *"Thus, says the LORD who made you and formed you from the womb."* He formed us and gave us gifts to fit together for His collective purpose.

"But one and the same Spirit works all these things, distributing to each one individually as He wills." 1 Corinthians 12:11. *"I will make you into a great nation, and I will bless you; I will make your name great, so that you will be a blessing. We are blessed to be a blessing."* Genesis 12:2

Proverbs 16:3 says He establishes our plans: *"Commit your works to the LORD, and your plans will be established." NASB*

And finally, Ephesians 2:10 declares that He created and equipped us to do good works: *"For we are His workmanship, created in Christ Jesus for good works, which God prepared beforehand that we should walk in them."*

He set order and authority in place for our good. He gives gifts and talents for the good of all. Total self-reliance, ignoring that God had anything to do with our gifts, abilities, talents, even our looks, inevitably leads to pride. It is good to have confidence but, be careful. Confidence is a wink away from arrogance, and arrogance walks our streets in direct defiance of the very God who gave us legs to walk on.

The idea of submitting to a higher being, of being dependent on anyone, is far removed from our society. The very word "submit" is taboo. We are supposed to fight for our "so-called" rights, no matter how offensive, how vulgar, or how far removed they are from God's law. Do people not know that God is the great equalizer? Who but a just God would recognize an unknown harlot alongside the great men of faith in the Bible? Rahab was credited as equal because of her faith. She had surrendered all that she knew, and all that she was, when she recognized and believed in the God of Israel. By faith she bowed in submission; by faith she was raised. Equality is not based on gender—equality is measured on the scales of righteousness. Whether man or woman, we all need Jesus to balance the scale. *Will they ever learn?*

The pervasive feminist ideals have so infected our culture—that to be a Christian woman living under the authority of God's Word, submitted to His will (and, if married, submitted to her husband) is seen as weak, when, in fact, the very opposite is true. To submit is a show of strength. Laying down our self-will takes a lot more courage than joining a march to proclaim it. Yet those who march for their rights—their right to choose, their right to deny rights to Christians—are the ones heralded as heroes. To say we are codependent on Christ is enough to get us shunned by society. Yes, the self-assertive syndrome is the acceptable trend of the day. Not only is it acceptable but applauded. Today's woman is pressed, pushed, and coerced to either fit this mold or be scorned. To acknowledge the accomplishments of women of faith would be self-defeating to their cause, so they shout loud enough to dispel what is written in the Bible and in the history books. But their shouts are not loud enough: Ruth, Joan of Arc, Huldah Buntain, and even our modern day hero Beverly LaHaye, who launched Concerned Women for America to combat the voice of the feminist promoting the decay of our Biblical principles while stomping on our moral virtues in the public square…are still heard.

How do we silence the cry of society, so those coming after us can hear the truth? How do we change the mindset of a self-driven society? *By not being conformed but transformed by the renewing of our mind.* By knowing that to be accepted by Him might mean being shunned by the world.

"And be not conformed to this world: but be ye transformed by the renewing of your mind, that ye may prove what is that good, and acceptable, and perfect, will of God." Romans 12:2

Most of us would purport that we have not succumbed to the subtle manipulation of Satan to conform to the world. *Let's see.*

The parallels of the self-willed woman and the codependent Christian woman are eerily similar. Like I mentioned earlier, self-will says, "I can do all things." Philippians 4:13 says *"I can do all things **through Christ which strengthens me**."* Big difference. But can the one watching distinguish the two? How does the world see us? Does God receive the glory in our successes? Time will reveal the truth. *If we are transformed, we will transform others.*

Ultimately, the self-willed woman *will* falter. Fear will prevail. One day this self-willed, pride-filled woman will look in the mirror and see the truth. The secret will go with her to her grave, unless she surrenders to Christ. Face-to-face with the ugly truth, yet unwilling to acknowledge that the platform of self-will, will leave her void, empty, fearful, and longing to be genuinely loved, longing for significance, longing to feel safe and protected, and longing to be understood. Pride will not allow her to utter the words that she was wrong. Pride will not allow her to acknowledge the futility of self-will. Pride will not allow her to declare that strength comes in surrender.

Pride and fear are powerful weapons used by the enemy to destroy us. Don't wear yourself out battling the enemy on your own. Seeking to be understood, seeking significance, without seeking Christ first, will not end well. Let the one watching see Christ and not you. *Be transformed.*

No matter what the world says, we were created to be dependent on Christ. He is our strength, our provider, and our life giver. Without Him, we can do nothing. Instead of being independent, embrace codependence. There is no shame. Instead of trusting in our own abilities, let's trust in Christ's ability.

The "Self Syndrome" does not stop there. Being self-supporting sounds good. We should trumpet a woman who can support herself and her family if that is how God leads. But for the Christian woman, there is no such thing as being self-supporting. We are *God-supported!*

Mathew 6:31-33 says, *"Therefore do not worry, saying, 'What shall we eat?' or 'What shall we drink?' or 'What shall we wear?' For after all these things the Gentiles seek. For your heavenly Father knows that you need all these things. But seek first the kingdom of God and His righteousness, and all these things shall be added to you."* What things? Anything you need to live life—food, clothing, shelter, comfort, peace…all things means *all* things.

Perhaps you are doing well. You've attained financial independence and achieved notable success. You have your dream home and your dream car. You might even be the CEO of a highly visible company or the author of a best seller. Don't get a big head! You did not do it on your own. Trust me, Satan will see to it that we get high praise for our accomplishments, and it will be hard not to bask in it. But watch out for the snare. Even the strongest women of faith can get caught in this one. We must pray before the success comes, pray that we see the very seed of pride before it takes root…before it ensnares us.

Now, the hardest attribute of the "Self Syndrome" to understand (and the one most likely to catch us off guard) is being *self-assertive*. I mentioned it briefly a little earlier; let's consider it further. "How does being self-assertive fit into any aspect of the Christian life?" we might ask. Christian women generally view being self-assertive as a derogatory trait, especially when considering the feminist movement—women who are loud and pushy, overbearing, speaking out for their own rights, demanding total equality, selfish extremists. Sounds harsh, doesn't it? But hold on. Speaking out for rights can be a good thing. I'm not for unfairness. In fact, the Bible is the true *fairness doctrine*. I'm simply for following the plan that God laid out for us in His Word—the plan that is best for us. So, before we make a ruling on being self-assertive, let's consider what God has to say about it. What does self-assertive mean from His perspective?

Proverbs 28:1 says the righteous are bold as a Lion: *"The wicked flee when no one pursues, But the righteous are bold as a lion."*

It means being bold in your righteous cause. Speaking out with confidence in Christ. It really means being *God-assertive*.

In Philippians 1:6 Paul proclaims, *"being confident of this very thing, that He who has begun a good work in you will complete it until the day of Jesus Christ."*

That simply means that Paul was sure of the result because He knew the person of Jesus Christ. Having confidence in Christ is a great asset for the Christian woman. We are called to achieve many things in our lives of service to Christ. We may be asked to speak at a lady's conference or speak before Congress, or, escort our husbands to a seminar, or host a seminar, or simply take the Little League for pizza. Whatever we are asked to do, we need to do it with the confidence of Christ, not with the confidence of the flesh, not asserting ourselves but asserting Christ.

Philippians 3:3 says, *"for we are the circumcision, who worship God in the Spirit, rejoice in Christ Jesus and have no confidence in the flesh."*

Paul continues throughout that chapter to explain that if anyone had reason to be confident in the flesh, to assert himself as having attained a position of greatness, he did. But instead, he professed that all he had attained in the flesh was counted as rubbish when compared to knowing Christ as his Lord. Did that mean he wasn't bold? Certainly not. Without boldness, we would shrink back from the task God has set before us. Without boldness, Paul would not have turned the world upside down. We would not have his letters of reproof or his instruction on what it means to love. It takes boldness for us to witness, just like it took boldness for him to witness…well, maybe he did need a bit more than we do. They were cutting people's heads off in his day. We might well find ourselves there soon, but today, all we really face is rejection and maybe a little humiliation if we, in fact, muster the boldness to witness to our neighbor, or our family, or to a crowd of unruly demonstrators. It takes being confident in Christ to be assertive for the gospel. But we must know the gospel! If we want to be heard, our audience must have a degree of respect for us. Now, I know we may be labeled as 'nuts' before we even open our mouths, but let's not give them a reason. If we are going to gain credibility and command their attention, we must be truthful, knowledgeable, and respectful in our assertions. I always say, "We don't want to lose our megaphone." If we get too crazy and appear too ridiculous, they simply won't hear us. It's a fine line. But without credibility we will have little effect. Know *what* you are talking about and know *who* you are talking about.

Before you judge me on this next one, hear me out. Having high self-esteem as a Christian woman means recognizing we are daughters of the Most High God. With that in mind, having that perspective, we should have high opinions of ourselves. Being daughters of the One who created life as we know it, joint heirs with Jesus Christ, puts us in pretty good company.

Romans 8:16-17 says, *"The Spirit Himself bears witness with our spirit that we are children of God and if children, then heirs—heirs of God and joint heirs with Christ, if indeed we suffer with Him, that we may also be glorified together."* That should bring smiles to our faces and a confident bounce to our steps—to know that our self-esteem is not established by mere human traits or abilities that deteriorate with time. It isn't dependent on outward beauty, but it is established by the very nature of God. Let's face it, we are not going to be 29 forever…or 39…or any of those "9's." The gray hairs and fine lines are inevitable. Of course, I intend to fight them every step of the way, but we certainly don't want our outward beauty to be our inner confidence, or it will diminish as our beauty fades. A little side note: Although men are attracted to external beauty, I have found that ultimately, they are more attracted to inner beauty. Think about it. How many of you find your mate drawn to you when he sees you tending to a sick baby or extending a hand to a friend in need? He sees the caring, gentle spirit of God working through you, and it's attractive. He sees true beauty—beauty that lasts. Age or disability cannot erase that beauty.

Now don't stop using the miracle age cream or start eating everything in sight. Take care of yourself. Give him your best. *I'm just saying...*

Neither should our self-esteem be dependent on our financial status, or even our marital status, which could be taken away instantly. A loss of a job. A car accident, death...it could all be gone. We cannot depend on such superficial things for our self-esteem. Our position afforded by the death and resurrection of Jesus is the foundation for our confidence, our strength, and our stability. So, we can have high self-esteem, not in who we are, but in *whose* we are.

"Charm is deceitful, and beauty is passing, but a woman who fears the Lord, she shall be praised." Proverbs 31:30

Now that we have a firm understanding of what being self-reliant, self-supporting, self-assertive, and having a high self-esteem means from a Christian perspective and what it affords us, let us use it to accomplish good.

"Therefore, do not cast away your confidence, which has great reward. For you have need of endurance, so that after you have done the will of God, you may receive the promise." Hebrews 10:35,36

Be strong in His might. Be bold in the Holy Spirit. Be empowered by the truth of His Word. It is our responsibility to change the mind of humanity, to save humanity. We are the light of the world. It is up to us to shine our light into the darkness, to bring understanding to the confused...to the misunderstood. Walk by the Spirit, being dependent on Christ. The soul of humanity depends on it. There are many causes to fight for, to stand up for...so stand up! If God calls you to a ministry, go for it. Be confident and bold in your commitments and convictions. Show the world that you are someone to be reckoned with. If an athlete, then be the best to the glory of God.

If you've never seen the old movie, *Chariots of Fire*, I encourage you to do so. It is based on a true account of several runners, who began their quest for glory in the Olympic games in 1924. One of these runners, Eric Liddle, was not only a runner but was also called to be a missionary to China. Mr. Liddle held strong convictions in his Christian faith, including keeping the Sabbath holy. In the movie, as in life, he made a stand for God, demonstrating to the world that although running was important to him, God was more important. His convictions for honoring God's commands would not be compromised. After years of training and competing and earning the coveted prize of being on Great Britain's Olympic team, Eric Liddle was soon faced with the most important decision of his life. His heat was to be run on a Sunday, the Lord's Day. Knowing the grave disappointment of his nation, and even knowing that God had destined him to run, Eric knew he had to withdraw from the games. He could not run on a Sunday. He could not dishonor God. He had to keep the Sabbath holy. He did withdraw from his race…but he *did* run, and it wasn't on a Sunday! I don't want to spoil the ending for you. Just know that the outcome was a clear demonstration of God's power to turn things in our favor when we stand by our convictions. It was a testimony and challenge for all Christians. Even one of his competitors encouraged him as he passed a note to Mr. Liddle, right before their race: *"It says in the good book that those who honor me I will honor."* God did honor Eric Liddle. Watch the movie. You will be inspired.

If singing is your gift, then do it to the glory of God. Before my husband was saved, he received a lot of recognition singing in secular settings, so when he got saved, he thought he had to stop singing. Wrong! God soon showed him that his *gift* was to be used for His glory. His gift of song has ministered to thousands.

Whatever God gifts you with, use it for the Kingdom. Be careful not to allow Satan to turn these gifts into something ugly, something that makes you prideful. He will try. Take no credit for yourself when put in a place of honor. Proclaim the name of Christ. Proclaim your dependence on Christ. Give Him the credit. It's not only beneficial for those who witness your triumph to recognize your dependence on Christ, but it is beneficial for *you* to recognize it.

Now if you're not athletically inclined, you're too timid to speak to your neighbor, let alone speak at a conference, and your singing is for your ears only, don't think you have nothing to offer. If you ask God, He will show you what your gift is. He will show you how you can help, minister, and inspire others to His glory. God has put in each of us those exact talents and abilities that we need to do the job He has called *us* to do. Don't feel diminished when surrounded by those with gifts and talents the world deems superior. Proverbs 31 tells us that a virtuous woman's worth is far above rubies. A wife with the patience to raise five children on her own, freeing up her husband for ministry, or a friend with the gift of encouragement who helps you face another day with hope, are both honorable and precious to the Lord. Whether we have been blessed with a pitch-perfect voice, the ability to persuade others in conversation, or are intellectually astute, the most excellent gift of all is love. 1 Corinthians 13 says that without love, we are nothing.

Ladies don't conform to a worldview that discredits the attributes of God, a worldview that denies the very existence of God. Stand up and be recognized *for* the glory of God, acknowledging your success comes from Him. Declare your dependence and then relentlessly pursue what He has ordained for you, and you will be amazed at what you can achieve. Rest in the security of knowing *whose* you are, not in *who* you are. Speak loudly with the voice of God. Live free, bound to Christ.

"And Joshua said to the people, 'Sanctify yourselves, for tomorrow the Lord will do wonders among you.'" Joshua 3:5

Chapter Seven — A Sound Mind

What defines a sound mind? How can we be sane in such an insane world? My definition of a sound mind: having the mental certainty and stability to discern and react to any idea or circumstance *without unfounded fear* and the ability to measure that idea or circumstance against Truth, to determine authenticity of fact versus fiction. Without Christ, it is impossible for anyone to possess these capabilities. Only Christ can cast out fear with His perfect love, and you must know the Truth to measure against it. There is no such thing as *your truth*. There is only *the Truth*. Without receiving His Holy Spirit—without having the mind of Christ—we cannot have a sound mind. Now I know I will face ridicule from the world for that statement. Let's face it: The problem with mankind without Christ, aside from living in sin, unforgiven, and bound for hell, is that man has a debased mind. A mind controlled by the sinful nature, corrupted by a distorted and perverted worldview, swayed by Satan's influences, is an unsound mind. A person without Christ can become so perverted in their thinking, so arrogant and prideful, that they esteem themselves higher than any being. It is all about them. *I think that is what got Lucifer into trouble.*

The prophet Isaiah warns against this attitude:

"Surely you have things turned around! Shall the potter be esteemed as the clay; For shall the thing made say of him who made it, 'He did not make me'? Or shall the thing formed say of him who formed it, 'He has no understanding'? Isaiah 29:16

In this chapter, we are going to explore the most important battle of all: the battle that takes place in the mind. The battleground of the mind is where we either succeed or fail. We either win or lose. For without a sound mind, we will not stand. *The first step to having a sound mind*—We must have on the helmet of salvation to protect our mind from the onslaught of fiery darts of deception, pride, or anything else that the world, or the devil, might throw at us.

If I have ever climbed on a soapbox, it has been for this issue. I implore you to give me your full attention. It is vital for your survival, for the survival of your marriage, for the survival of your ministry. Our minds must be guarded and protected against the deceptions and temptations Satan will bring to us at the early stages of our thought processes—the battle of self-will verses God's will. I know this place all too well. I know firsthand the danger of allowing your mind to become weak and vulnerable to the attack of Satan. The revelation, the encouragement, and perhaps the wisdom that I am about to impart comes from my own miraculous journey that took me from the edge of death, by suicide, to the very pinnacle of life in Jesus Christ. I believe personal experience is the key to effectively addressing a topic with authority and credibility. Perhaps that is the very reason God has allowed me to go through such heartache…such insurmountable circumstances. Trust me, I can sympathize with the broken hearted, with the one whose spirit has been crushed, with the one who no longer has hope. I have experienced the inner turmoil of the torment of Satan, barely clinging to hope—until I couldn't. I reached the point of no return, yet here I am. I planned my death thirty-seven years ago, yet here I am. I know what I'm talking about. I can empathize. Hebrews 4:15 says, *"For we do not have a High Priest who cannot sympathize with our weaknesses, but was in all points tempted as we are, yet without sin."* Jesus knew through His becoming a man and being tempted in all things, He could understand the seduction of Satan's temptations used against man. Man would know that Jesus himself could sympathize with them. Only then could the Word be poured out precisely and effectively to address any temptation or sin we would face. He could answer any question we might have. He has all the answers.

I thank God that I am sitting here writing this book today, for without Him, you would never know my story. My sons would not have known their mother, and my Father would not have a daughter to shine His light into this dark world. My struggle to overcome depression was almost lost. In my early twenties, I found myself in a dark place, but no one knew it. My secret was well hidden. No one knew how I longed for death. How I longed to be where I was loved, in the arms of my Father. I had reached the point where I felt no one loved me. My youth had been crushed when time and again my mother would abandon us, only to return weeks or months later, collect us from whatever relative had taken us in, pack us up, and move us to another city—a city where no one knew her weaknesses. Adultery along with physical and mental abuse told me I was not a good wife. I was not a woman who could capture the love and faithfulness of her husband. I was not worthy. I was weak. I was a failure as a wife and mother. My sons would be better off without me. I was soothed only by thoughts of running my car off a bridge, sinking slowly beneath the water, or cutting my wrist, with my blood slowly leaving my body. I could say more, but I won't. Once I was there—where I thought death meant peace——only a miracle could bring me out. Only God could bring deliverance, and I praise Him every day that He did. His light of truth revealed the lie. I thank Him every day that through the years and through my many trials, He has taught me to count it all joy! James tells us, *"My brethren, count it all joy when you fall into various trials, knowing that the testing of your faith produces patience. But let patience have its perfect work, that you may be perfect and complete, lacking nothing."* What a thought——to be lacking in nothing! The first step to having that promise fulfilled in our lives is to be reconciled to God through accepting what Jesus did for us on the cross of Calvary. Once we have made that declaration of faith, then and only then can His grace cover our sin and shame.

The second step to having that promise fulfilled—to be lacking in nothing—is to walk in the fullness of the Holy Spirit. You see, I was saved, but I was weak. I was still walking in the flesh without power. I was blind to who I was in Christ. I had listened to Satan's lie that I was unlovable for so long, I couldn't hear the truth. I thought the beauty of my youth would win me love, but even that had failed me. I didn't understand that it is only through the ministry (guidance, wisdom, power) of the Holy Spirit that we see, stand, and succeed. Only through the ministry of the Holy Spirit can we begin the process of restoration and renewal. Only through the ministry of the Holy Spirit can we start the journey toward having a sound mind. It wasn't the antidepressants or the counseling sessions that saved me; it was the love of the Father, the love of the Son, and the ministry of the Holy Spirit.

If you have ever suffered, or are suffering, from anxiety or depression, I invite you to journey with me to that place of peace that surpasses all understanding. Let me start with a couple of promises.

"Peace I leave with you, My peace I give to you; not as the world gives do I give to you. Let not your heart be troubled, neither let it be afraid." John 14:27

"Be anxious for nothing, but in everything by prayer and supplication, with thanksgiving, let your requests be made known to God; and the peace of God, which surpasses all understanding, will guard your hearts and minds through Christ Jesus." Philippians 4:6-7

The road to sanity for one who has tasted the bitterness of the insane is traveled with much uncertainty. God alone can bring order and direction to a confused and dismayed mind. God alone can bring hope to one who is hopeless. God alone can dispel fear from the one who is tormented.

"For God has not given us a spirit of fear, but of power and of love and of a sound mind." 2 Timothy 1:7 was my salvation during the time I was crippled by depression. I was crippled by the deception of Satan. I believed the only way I would feel loved was to go home to the Father. At a time when I had accepted all Satan's lies, *I heard the Truth.*

I had planned my suicide: I laid out the pills and the razor, left my sons with my mom the night before, and then decided to go to church one last time…*I thought*. I sat there on the pew in a daze, not hearing anything, really, until the preacher said these words: "There is someone here today who is about to take their life, and God wants you to know that He did not send His Son for you to die, but that you would live."

The words broke into my silence and penetrated my heart. I was surprised by simply *feeling* something again. It was as if the Lord had touched a part of me that had been dead for years. Tears flowed. I stood and went forward and confessed my plan to take my life that very afternoon. It wasn't easy. That was the first step of a thousand steps required to get on the other side. I still cried almost every day. In fact, my boss forced me to go to counseling after two weeks of crying in the office, so I went. I promptly told the counselor that I had simply wanted to go home to my Father who loved me. She promptly called the psychiatric ward of the hospital next door and told them to get a bed ready. I was a danger to myself. At first, it was soothing to think of surrendering all my efforts and simply conceding to being insane, lying in a bed drugged, with no demands, nothing to confront…and then the Spirit woke me up. He reminded me of what God had just done. He whispered a warning: *If they lock you in, you won't get out.* I was alerted to the consequence of giving up. I literally changed my tune. My mind was alert. I told them of my experience at church and that I knew the value of my life. I would not leave my sons. They released me into the care of a friend. It was a narrow escape. Who knows where I would be today if the Holy Spirit hadn't warned me, if He hadn't given me the words to say?

The deception was so great, and the pain was so deep that my road back to sanity took years. The thought of suicide reared itself again and again, with every hurt, every disappointment, every failed attempt at being loved...*but God kept me!* His love kept me. My eyes were opened to the love of friends and the love of my sons. And yes, eventually, five years after that fateful day, I met the love of my life, Frank. It took me moving from California to Houston, Texas, but it happened, and in 1986, we were married.

Years ago, when Frank first started in full-time ministry, singing with a gospel group called *The Sound*, there was a song they sang called *"Daystar"* with a line that says, *"We are all groping in the darkness, haunted by years of past defeat."* I think that line is the best way to explain how it felt to climb out of deep depression. I felt like I was groping in the darkness, stumbling over my past with each step I took. The light of Jesus led me out. It is the *only* way out. Being on the other side, it's clear to see that if you are in darkness, you need a light. If you keep stumbling over your past, you need to remove it. That is exactly what Jesus is and what Jesus does.

"Again, a new commandment I write to you, which thing is true in Him and in you, because the darkness is passing away, and the true light is already shining." 1 John 2:8

Why did Jesus come to be our light to show us the way out of darkness? Why would God forgive and forget our sins?

"For God so loved the world that He gave His only begotten Son, that whoever believes in Him should not perish but have everlasting life." John 3:16

Love is the answer; love is the reason. And as I said, understanding the love of God and *accepting* the grace He offers *is* the first step to having a sound mind.

To some of you, this may seem elementary. I understand that. But I tell you, we have an enemy who is relentless in bombarding our minds. It is this very elementary truth that may just save your life like it did mine. The foundation of our faith is what keeps us stable in an unstable world. The love of God towards us, our salvation in Jesus Christ, and the power we have in the Holy Spirit is our anchor. It is how we overcome. It is how we stay sane. It is how we get back from the edge of insanity. The Word tells us to take every thought captive—to choose to keep it if it's good or dismiss it if it's harmful.

If your husband says something that hurts and offends you, (and trust me, he will,) remember what he's made of: *dust,* just like you and me.

Frank is very purposeful with his words, carefully presenting his position in a logical way, hoping to avoid conflict. Often compassion is overshadowed in the heat of a matter, in the pursuit of getting to the facts. It's not that he isn't compassionate. He cries easily and often when seeing the pain of others, but in debate, he is like most men—no drama, just the facts, ma'am. Now I am very logical as well, but *in general*, like most women, I tend to operate with sensitivity when confronting a potentially volatile situation. So, although I might get stoned in the public square for saying this, men and women are different—you know, the whole Mars and Venus thing. Don't hold onto the hurt of harsh words spoken in the heat of anger. Don't nurture your pain to full growth, allowing your imagination to make it more than what it was. Satan is in the business of doing just that. Make the choice to dismiss it before it destroys you, before your relationship suffers. Dwell on the good. Do not allow Satan to rule your mind.

"Finally, brethren, whatever things are true, whatever things are noble, whatever things are just, whatever things are pure, whatever things are lovely, whatever things are of good report, if there is any virtue and if there is anything praiseworthy—meditate on these things." Philippians 4:8.

When we take our thoughts captive and dwell on the good, victory comes. I believe some marriages fail over things imagined rather than things that really happened. We are going to have conflict and adversity in relationships. There will be things that need to be addressed and worked on, but let's not allow a small issue to explode into a mountain because of our imagination. Let's not allow a hurtful word said in anger to build into a reason for all-out war. And let's not allow that hurtful word be a vehicle for resurrecting every hurtful word or action ever done against us. In case you don't know, that, ladies, is unscriptural. In my first few years of marriage to Frank, perhaps more than any other scriptures, 1 Corinthians 13:5 and 1 Peter 4:8 are the ones that saved our marriage. And they just may save yours.

"Love does not take into account a wrong suffered."
1 Corinthians 13:5 NASB

"And above all things have fervent love for one another, for "love will cover a multitude of sins." 1 Peter 4:8

Love does not remember a wrong suffered. Would we want Jesus to remember the wrongs He suffered at our hands? At our actions? At our words? Would we want to beg again and again for forgiveness every day, for sins we committed last week or last year or ten years ago? No, of course we wouldn't. Heaven forbid! *We could not stand under the weight of condemnation. We would never be able to lift our heads.*

Ladies, we are to love, forgive, *and forget* the way Christ loves, forgives, and forgets. If we want mercy, we must show mercy. If we want forgiveness, we must forgive. And if we want our sins covered and remembered no more, we must not remember the sins of those who hurt us. It took Frank a few years to overcome his outbursts of anger, but, praise God, he did. I rest daily in the strong comfort and love of a mature Christian husband and I praise God for the truth and power of His Word that kept us. I know it's a tall order, a lot to ask, but we ask that of God every day. He does it, and we can do it. We are to address the troubles of each day. The conflicts, the differences of opinion, the wrongs suffered from days past should never be considered again. I am certain that those two scriptures literally saved my marriage. I would not allow myself to remember previous wrongs suffered. I measured my response to each new conflict against that sole conflict, forgetting the past.

The second step to having a sound mind is submitting to the Spirit—allowing the Holy Spirit the liberty to control your actions and your reactions, giving you the power to have self-control in all things…and that means *ALL* things. It might seem impossible, but it is not. It is a discipline, however, that we must commit to and practice daily.

Let's look at four areas that we might have trouble controlling. If we consider them now, we may not have to consider them when face-to-face with the challenge. We may be able to avoid the challenge altogether. The first area, we've already touched on—controlling our thoughts, bringing every thought captive. When Jesus addressed the issue of adultery, He said that if a man looks upon a woman and lusts after her, he has already committed adultery in his heart. God lets us know how serious the thought process is. We have all heard the saying, "Look, but don't touch." I believe Jesus is telling us that if we look, the thought is planted, and it won't be long before we touch. Once we start down the path of looking, the act is not far behind. If we are entertaining the thoughts, we already have a problem. Impure thoughts are the path to destruction. Sooner or later, our thoughts lead to actions. Satan knows this all too well. You may say, "I'm not having lustful thoughts." Amen! *Or at least not today.* But you may be thinking your husband is. Caution: Don't let your thoughts run wild. Do not make unwarranted accusations based on speculation. Making accusations, without proof, is dangerous. It is your choice. Don't respond to *what you imagine.* If you suspect it, ask him. Even if he is not honest, remember God sees all things, and He loves both of you too much to keep it hidden. At some point, sin is always exposed.

The second area we may have trouble controlling is our emotions. No way! Yes, way! The Lord speaks out very clearly in Proverbs against outbursts of anger. When tempers are flaring and hearts are hurting, there is a high probability that we will say or do something that we will regret. You cannot take it back. We must guard ourselves against unruly emotions. Walk by the Spirit, speaking words that edify and lift the other person to a better place. Words of correction spoken in love bring reconciliation. Words of correction spoken in anger lead to contention.

The third area, and inevitably the hardest to control, is the tongue.

"But no man can tame the tongue. It is an unruly evil, full of deadly poison." James 3:8

The tongue can be a damaging instrument, bringing irreparable harm. I pray daily for God to shut my mouth that I might not speak anything to bring reproach upon Him. Abusive, destructive words kill the person we say them to, and they kill us as well. How many times have you wished you could take back the ugly words you said to someone you dearly cared for? It's time we learn that silence is truly golden. Be led by the Spirit. Ask God for the wisdom to know when to speak and when to be quiet. Ask for the wisdom to know what to say and how to say it. Speak to others the way you want to be spoken to. If harsh words are used against you, refuse to allow them to taint your heart.

Finally, I want to touch on the fourth area we might have a hard time controlling: the stomach. To put it simply, we should be masters over our stomachs and not allow it to master us. Isn't that what the Word says? The reason this seems to be an area that is hard to overcome is because we have a hard time overcoming the other three areas. Nervous or anxious eating, comfort eating if you will, is the reason some of us have a hard time with overeating. We are convinced that we can soothe our anxiety, our hurt, our stresses with comfort food. Now where do you think that lie came from? You guessed it: Satan once again.

Circumstance rules our minds and bodies: what we think, what we do, what we say, *and* what we eat. It shouldn't be. I'm not going to get into a long dissertation about being fat or thin, but I do want to remind us that the body is the dwelling place of the Holy Spirit, the very temple of God. We are responsible for keeping it strong and healthy and fit. How else will we have the energy and vitality to carry out the work of the Lord? And yes, to the best of our abilities, we are responsible for keeping ourselves desirable for our mates. In the past twelve months, I lost twenty pounds and joked with my youngest son how wonderful it was to go to the closet to dress without needing a Xanax! (*It was a joke!*) I have never taken a Xanax in my life, but you get my point. Well, maybe not; maybe I'm the only one who hated my clothes being so tight that I never wanted to get out of my sweatpants and go out. However, I don't really believe that. I suspect many of you, like me, have gone on diets and perhaps lost a few pounds and as a result, gained a sense of achievement. We felt good, looked good, and yes, could slip into those jeans with a little satisfaction. The opposite of that is when our self-control dwindles, and our appetites increase.

Unwanted weight gain can leave us a little discouraged and perhaps even depressed and, dare I say, not as willing to put on that tight-fitting laced nightie that our husband loves to see us in. (You can redact this part if you like.) I know not every woman has a wild, passionate love affair with her husband, but I do. If you don't, I recommend it. Don't deprive yourself or your husband (perhaps future husband) and hold fast to your commitment to be your best. Don't allow your stomach to dictate your state of well-being. Trust me, I know it's hard. Our lives are bombarded daily with overwhelming trials. But in the face of the trials, we must learn to feed on God's Word, not food. Find our nourishment and comfort in the Holy Spirit, not suffer Death by Chocolate! Don't feel bad if you have succumbed; I have too. I'm "preaching to the choir," as they say. I simply want to encourage us to strive for healthier bodies and just maybe, a more victorious, fulfilled lifestyle. Being overweight isn't what makes your life unfulfilled, but lack of self-control is. Constant disappointment in ourselves will crush our spirit. My biggest heartache is in not pleasing God. It is God's will for us to be in good physical and mental health. God instructs us to have self-control in this very area. There is a reason it was mentioned in the Bible. There is a reason Satan keeps using it.

I challenge all of us to examine the areas of our lives that are out of control. Look inside and look in the mirror. What are we being ruled by? Ask God for the wisdom to see your weakness and ask Him to give you the strength to overcome it. Be disciplined in the study of the Word. Fast and pray. Deny yourself. Be a living sacrifice. God will reward.

Once we begin to live under the influence of the Holy Spirit, we will see a difference in our ability to have self-control, and our lives will operate on a more even keel, no longer moved by impulse but moved by the Spirit. Every victory empowers us for the next victory. We become more aware of the snares and more equipped to escape them. But make no mistake, the more we pursue victory in each of these areas, the more Satan will pursue us. The present condition of our society is appalling. We are continually inundated with temptations. Television, billboards, magazine ads all serve as vehicles to lure and seduce us into lusting after the pleasures and false appeasements of this world. Food, sex, alcohol, prescription drugs, or simply attaining a higher standard of living, are presented as rewards for a job well done or as comfort for a job undone. "Go ahead, you deserve it, whatever the reason. Indulge yourself. It will help." It's no wonder opioid addiction, alcoholism, and even eating disorders are rampant in our society, not to mention the crushing weight of credit card debt. Media suggestions are very powerful, and Satan is at the root of most of them. I pray that you will not be trapped by his deception. Only God can deliver us from such powerful snares. Only the Holy Spirit can empower us with the ability to see and the ability to say "no." Conflict and confusion confront us at every corner. If we are blind and powerless, failure is certain. Mentally weakened, we become vulnerable to the enemy. He attacks with a vengeance. Don't be destroyed. Don't give him the victory any longer. Stand firm. Walk daily in the discipline of self-control. Look at our example—Jesus Christ, who is the epitome of self-control. Reflect on His life. Christ had complete self-control in each of the four areas, and we can, too.

Love, power, and a sound mind are what God has ordained for us. We cannot allow Satan to steal them. Remember: The first step was learning to accept the love of God and the grace and forgiveness He offers. Being certain of His love, His grace, and His mercy removes the burden of guilt and shame and casts out our fears. We are freed from the past, freed in the present, and free to look to the future. Then we saw how we have the power to have self-control in all things through the Holy Spirit, overcoming Satan's lies and seductions with supernatural sight and strength. Now let's look at the last critical element in our quest for a sound mind: wisdom.

A SOUND MIND

Proverbs 3 encourages us to seek out and find wisdom. So how do we obtain wisdom? The answer is simple. The personality of wisdom is the very personality of Christ. It is said that when you marry someone, you eventually take on the characteristics of that person. When we accept Christ, we marry into His family. If the rule follows, we would take on the personality and characteristics of Christ, and Christ is wisdom. The reason we take on the characteristics of our mate is because we spend so much time with him, so the rule would only apply to our taking on the characteristics of Christ—His wisdom—if we spend a lot of time with Him.

Proverbs 3 tells us that the worth of wisdom is far above jewels, that it is trustworthy, and that it will bring us happiness and prosperity. Wisdom provides sustenance, robes us in righteousness, and the light of wisdom never goes out. When we seek and attain wisdom, we attain the very nature and personality of Christ. We seek wisdom in prayer and in His Word.

I asked the Lord for wisdom every day for the first thirty years of my marriage to Frank. We just celebrated thirty-three years. I read Proverbs every day for those first thirty years and even used the word "wisdom" for my password when I got my first e-mail account. I was serious about seeking wisdom. When Frank first went into ministry, knowing he would be leaving a high-paying job with Hertz for a job that paid $300 dollars a week, I told him that I would be the Proverbs 31 wife and would make a living so he would not have to worry about the money. In other words, I would be *buying a field and planting a vineyard* (my next book). He was free to pursue God's leading.

And that is what I did. God blessed my career far more than I could have ever imagined when I made that declaration. Now, retired from banking, as a pastor's wife and author, I recently found myself reflecting on the success I had. I wondered how a poor girl from West Virginia, whose parents never finished high school, could have had such success. The next morning at 5:00 am, the Lord woke me up and said, *"You asked me for wisdom for thirty years, and I gave it to you."* Wow! It's amazing. God says to ask, and He will give it to us. When we do…He does.

I remember that prior to my banking career, when Frank was singing with *The Sound*, I had a short stint of being a stay-at-home mom but still needed to earn a living. I was given an opportunity to do desktop publishing from home, whatever that was. It was at a time when the floppy disk was the innovation of the day. (I know, it's funny *and shows my age.*) Anyway, I had a three-inch book to tell me all about it. Frank said he would help me when he got home from his trip. The rent wouldn't wait until he got home. I placed my hand on that book and simply stated that I had the mind of Christ and that He could figure out any computer program. I opened the book, *Ventura Publishing*, and the rest was history. I finished the layout of ten pages and earned rent and grocery money, and a little extra. Frank could not believe it.

You see, the beginning of wisdom is to fear (reverence) the Lord. To reverence the Lord is to know and honor Him, and to know Him is to know His Word. His Word gives us knowledge of Him, and the Spirit anoints the knowledge producing wisdom, transforming our minds into the mind of Christ. If we apply it to every aspect of our lives, we will have success.

I'm sure most of you have read Proverbs 31 at one time or another. You know the one—the chapter that women are supposed to model their lives after (and, by the way, we should). The virtuous woman has the very characteristics of wisdom. Her worth is far above rubies. Sound familiar? The virtuous woman has the same value as wisdom! They are one and the same. Wisdom and virtue lift us above our circumstances, allowing us to see life from a higher perspective. We are no longer mired in a milky, day-to-day existence, but soar in the understanding of who we are as mothers, wives, women, and as daughters of God, confident in our pursuits. A virtuous, wise woman knows she can do all things through Christ who strengthens her. When the wind and rains come, when the storm is raging, we are not dismayed. We do not stumble. We do not shrink back. When faced with an impossible task, it becomes possible.

"However, we speak wisdom among those who are mature, yet not the wisdom of this age, nor of the rulers of this age, who are coming to nothing. But we speak the wisdom of God in a mystery, the hidden wisdom which God ordained before the ages for our glory, which none of the rulers of this age knew; for had they known, they would not have crucified the Lord of glory. But as it is written:

'Eye has not seen, nor ear heard, nor have entered into the heart of man the things which God has prepared for those who love Him.'

But God has revealed them to us through His Spirit. For the Spirit searches all things, yes, the deep things of God. For what man knows the things of a man except the spirit of the man which is in him? Even so no one knows the things of God except the Spirit of God. Now we have received, not the spirit of the world, but the Spirit who is from God, that we might know the things that have been freely given to us by God. These things we also speak, not in words which man's wisdom teaches but which the Holy Spirit teaches, comparing spiritual things with spiritual.

But the natural man does not receive the things of the Spirit of God, for they are foolishness to him; nor can he know

A SOUND MIND

them, because they are spiritually discerned. But he who is spiritual judges all things, yet he himself is rightly judged by no one. For who has known the mind of the Lord that he may instruct Him? But we have the mind of Christ." 1 Corinthians 2:6-16

We can know the very thoughts of God. We can have a sound mind because God has a sound mind and allows us free access to it. We can draw from the very depths of God's Spirit the wisdom needed to succeed in this unstable world. I approach every situation in my life with the understanding that the Spirit that dwells in me knows all things and can accomplish all things. There is nothing He can't do, so there is nothing I can't do. I simply need to ask, whether it's learning a computer program, managing a budget, or writing a ministry book for women.

Accepting Christ, receiving His grace, living in His love without fear, controlled by His Spirit, walking in His wisdom, equipped with His virtue, soaring above our circumstances, having the mind of Christ...*powerful!*

"For God has not given us a spirit of fear, but of power and of love and of a sound mind." 2 Timothy 1:7

CHAPTER EIGHT – YIELDED, BUT NOT FORGOTTEN

Submit, serve, and obey: I think I've mentioned these words a time or two. Usually the word "woman" can be found in the same sentence with any of the three. They are words that define our role and reflect our character as Christian women, *and they should*. God has called us all into a submissive role, a role of servanthood. This should be the very core of who we are. However, He has also called us His daughters and joint heirs with Jesus. So, keep smiling as we look at the big picture.

There are other words that define who we are as Christian women—the words:

> **Valuable** – Proverbs 31:10
> **Trustworthy** – Proverbs 31:11
> **Praiseworthy** – Proverbs 31:30-31
> **Wise** – Proverbs 31:26

I dare say, this descriptive list is a little less familiar to us, and perhaps a little less mentioned in the hushed conversations of men. Our being valuable or wise may even be somewhat of a new concept around our own households. But take it from me, no, take it *from God*—that if you lead a life yielded and submitted to God in humility and service, our children and husbands will call us blessed. As in all things with God, there is a perfect order. Our blessing comes through serving. Our work as servants makes us valuable. In our obedience, we are found to be trustworthy. In our humility, we are praised. And in our submission, wisdom is declared. If we are willing to yield completely to that perfect plan that God has ordained for us, daily dying to self, His lavish rewards will astound us. The recognition that we secretly desire from man will pale next to the honor that God will bestow on us. God has not forgotten the sacrifices we have made. He did not turn His head and look the other way when we bowed low to pick up "donkey dung." He was there with us in the countless hours we spent alone. His heart hurt every time our hearts hurt. Whatever we do in secret, however we serve, is seen by Him. Nothing escapes God.

As we put on the cloak of humility, He clothes us with honor. As we put our hands to the distaff to clothe our family, He clothes us in purple and fine linen. As we submit to the role of servants, He elevates us to the place of royalty. He declares us His daughters and His heirs.

"The Spirit Himself bears witness with our spirit that we are children of God, and if children, then heirs—heirs of God and joint heirs with Christ, if indeed we suffer with Him, that we may also be glorified together." Romans 8:16-17

We have His promise of rewards now and His promise of rewards later. Proverbs 31 tells us that the value of a virtuous women is far above rubies. It declares that a woman who fears the Lord shall be praised. Our children and our husbands will praise us. Others will praise us. Our works will praise us. Even those who honor our husbands will praise us. His peers will acknowledge and admire our virtue; they will proclaim to him that we are worthy of praise. And ladies, the very ones who he has ministered to, the ones who we may have envied and been jealous of, yes, even those who took him from us, will acknowledge our sacrifice and commend us. We may be yielded, but we are not forgotten.

It may take years before our husbands rise to the occasion and honor us the way God intends, but the Word does not lie. It *will* happen. Early in our ministry, I often thought that if Frank was going to honor me, it would surely not be on this side of heaven. Right or wrong, I longed for his recognition. I knew he appreciated what I did; I just didn't fit into the schedule. His mind was too consumed by the moment to have me in it. He was always too pressed with the task at hand to mention me...*so I thought*. But as I put my thoughts to pen twenty-six years ago (the initial writing of this book), I easily recalled the many times that he had credited me with being the support he needed to keep going, saying the very reason he could be out there doing God's work was because of me. Looking back even today, after almost thirty years of full-time ministry, I realize that in those early days, I gave away my blessing of praise because I didn't think it was enough. He did give me credit, and he still gives me credit, way more than I deserve. I encourage you to take a minute, reflect, and remember. You might be surprised. And if you are newly married, new to full-time ministry, or when you do marry, don't give away your blessings. Listen closely. Journal your journey. *If* you are the Proverbs 31 woman, the honor will come, when you are not looking for it. My advice: Don't look for it. Let it surprise you.

I recall a day at the beginning of our ministry when Frank was substituting for our Sunday School teacher. At the end of class, he called everyone to attention. He said he wanted to share something with them. He opened the book to Proverbs 31 and began to read. When he concluded, he looked at me with deep admiration as he said that the words defined his wife and that he wanted to honor her before the class. My mouth closed and my heart opened. That was not the only time he did that. Over the years, he has often expressed his admiration for me. Maybe some of you experience acknowledgement and admiration daily from those you serve…others have yet to hear it. *If you see something, say something.* Offer praise for a job well done.

Why do you think God declared His promise of praise? His reward of recognition? His declaration of honor for those who honor Him? Because His heart overflows with joy when His creation praises Him, and He created us in His image. He knew our hearts would, too. To acknowledge and honor someone is simply an expression of love. And we all want to be loved. We all want to know that someone loves us—that someone sees us. It's not about receiving praise; it's about praise satisfying our need for love.

God has not forgotten you. His indwelling Spirit within your husband, within your friends, within your children, will cause them to rise up and fulfill this promise to you. God's Word promises us that a woman who fears the Lord will be praised. He does not lie. He understands our need to feel loved. He understands the quiet joy we feel when love is expressed through an act or word of recognition. Praise isn't something we seek, but when it comes, recognize it as a gift from our Father to encourage us to keep going. 1 Samuel 2:30 says, *"...those who honor Me, I will honor."* Honor Him in obedience with a spirit of humility and a heart of submission, and He will honor you because He loves you. Why do you say, "Son, I'm so proud of you. What a beautiful act of kindness you showed by carrying her bags to the car."? Or "Son, I'm so proud of you for volunteering at the homeless shelter."? Or, when our five-year-old looks to us, innocently longing for approval after sweeping the leaves from one side of the patio to the other, why do we say, "I'm so proud of you for helping Mommy. What a great job you did!"? It's innate in all of us. We feel good because our child feels good. You are His child. It takes a while to figure this one out but think about this: *"His lord said to him, 'Well done, good and faithful servant; you were faithful over a few things, I will make you ruler over many things. Enter into the joy of your lord.'"* Matthew 25:21. Don't we all long to hear that? He wants you to hear it more than you want to hear it.

Like I said, it is innate in all of us to want to be accepted and seen by others. It says we are loved. Through the work of the Holy Spirit, I eventually came to understand that my Father loved and cherished me deeply. It didn't matter if man did. I would one day hear, "Well done." Oh, I still relish recognition. I still relish receiving a Hallmark card and a box of chocolates. It does feel good, but, praise God, I have reached a point where the emotional swings of spiritual puberty that had been my "MO" for so many years gave way to spiritual maturity. I can look past the disappointments, the heartache, and hurt feelings of being misunderstood, of feeling unloved, of not being recognized, because I know that one day my Father will recognize me.

The gift of the fullness of the fruits of the Spirit—love, patience, kindness, peace, contentment—comes when we have suffered through the growth pains of spiritual puberty to spiritual maturity. This reward (the reward of maturity in Christ, the reward of being perfected into His image) is the best reward of all. I am not saying I am there yet. I have not arrived. Trust me; none of us will get there this side of heaven. But amid adversity, during the storm,

I am at rest. I am at peace. Some rewards are tangible, and some are intangible. All are from God. It is His will to give us the desires of our heart. He desires to honor us, if we will but honor Him.

In October of 2013, the Lord gave me a new calling. The day Frank was ordained as Senior Pastor of Freedom Fellowship was the day the Lord called me to a different work. I remember it well. It rests deep within my soul.

I didn't want to go on the platform when Frank asked me to go with him. I was satisfied with my place of "shadow serving." But I took his hand and stood next to him. After the ordination service, Pastor Bates turned to me and asked, "Lib, do you want to say something?" My first thought was *"No way."* I was stunned for a minute. Then the Lord spoke and said, *"Take the mic, take a step, and speak."* I did. To everyone's shock and *my surprise,* I boldly proclaimed my commitment to my new role. For ten minutes I walked the platform declaring God's power. The new anointing was clear to everyone in the sanctuary, and it was clear to me. Looking back now, more than five years later, to that fateful day when God called me out from the shadows, I realize that serving in the shadows was *a lot* easier then serving in the spotlight…but I wouldn't change a thing. To walk in His power and be a force for truth is a rich blessing, and worth the burden…worth the fight.

I had no idea what that day would put in motion. I would soon learn that not everyone would be happy about my new place of service. For me and Frank, it was the most beautiful gift God could have given us. Week after week I was standing next to him on the platform, speaking what God had given me to encourage anyone with a burden to come to the altar for prayer, exhorting and proclaiming God's power and love under the anointing of the Holy Spirit. The atmosphere was alive and exciting and beautiful. Frank and I were together, under the anointing, side by side, ministering to the body. The church family was alive. The Spirit was alive and working and flowing. Women and men came to me and rejoiced in the work God had done, hardly believing the transformation in my life. I remember two women in our congregation whose husbands had once been pastors, but had both fallen into adultery, telling me how beautiful it was to see us working together as a team. Our marriage, our unity, was unifying for the church, for other couples... except for a few *men*. Now, I wasn't preaching or teaching men; that's important to know. I was spending five minutes exhorting and building our faith before we went to prayer. And before I ever stepped on the platform, I labored in the Word and in prayer for what God wanted to say in those five minutes. Then, I submitted to the leading of His Holy Spirit.

I read the names of our family members who needed prayer and opened the altar for individuals to come forward. However minimal my role was, over time, the undercurrent of a few who believed that women (or should I say, "believing that I") should be quiet in the church, took its toll. I say they believed that *I* should stay quiet because there was never a word said against the previous pastor's wife, and they clapped and shouted for other women in our pulpit——women who were ordained, women who led worship, *women who had not been "corrupted by the corporate world."* What do you say to that? They assumed that because I had authority over men in the corporate world, I would exert authority over them. They were wrong. My husband thought the giftings and knowledge God had given me in my twenty-five-year finance career could be an asset for the church, these few men saw it as a detriment. All I wanted to do was submit to God, submit to the call, and submit to my husband, but they wanted me to submit to them. They wanted my husband to submit to them. Frank heard them out, and he searched it out. His position was God's position. God said He would pour out His Spirit upon *all* flesh. After all, had the apostles been ordained? Had Lydia? Priscilla? Anna? Deborah? Phoebe? Mary Magdalene? He used them all. They proclaimed His truth, supported His ministry, and started churches.

"And it shall come to pass in the last days, says God, That I will pour out of My Spirit on all flesh; Your sons and your daughters shall prophesy, your young men shall see visions, your old men shall dream dreams. And on My menservants and on My maidservants, I will pour out My Spirit in those days; And they shall prophesy." Acts 2:17-18

YIELDED, BUT NOT FORGOTTEN

I told Frank I would step down, sit down, and be quiet. I didn't want to be the problem. Even though I knew God had called me to do it, I knew He would understand if I just closed my mouth and went back to "shadow serving." My husband did not agree. Our board did not agree. The church as a whole would not have agreed. So, I kept doing what God had called me to do—be a helpmeet to my husband in whatever way he needed. Yet my spirit was crushed. The Holy Spirit in me had been quenched, not by my will or my choosing, but by a few men *with good intentions*…and I mean that. I fully believe they had good intentions.

In January of 2016, I launched our Wednesday café night to enhance the opportunity for all to attend our Wednesday service. For eight months, I pretty much did it on my own, other than a few sweet folks helping me set up and serve. Now, these same men loved when I was in the kitchen serving, and I loved that, too! I loved the folks filing by as I served up my latest creation. I loved wherever God put me. I loved cooking for the "family". But God doesn't just call us to the kitchen. He calls us to where He can best use us, and then equips and empowers us to fulfill that call.

I would have laid down my life for those men. I still would. I love them. They thought they were doing the right thing. Still I was crushed. Sometimes I had to leave the house so Frank wouldn't see me cry, so he wouldn't see how broken I was. I didn't understand why they didn't understand. These were men of the Word. Didn't they know that Jesus had first appeared to a woman after His resurrection and commanded her to *"go and tell"* the others that she had seen Him? Talk about encouraging words of faith! If He could use her at a time in history when women had no credibility as witnesses, why couldn't He have chosen me now? There were women in the Upper Room when the Spirit fell. Why couldn't the Spirit fall on me? I didn't understand why they didn't understand. I was scrutinized every minute in every way. This book is not long enough to tell you the full affect it had on me and my husband. My liberty in the Spirit was quenched. I prayed for God to change the calling, but...He didn't. Frank was the worship leader and pastor/preacher. I led our altar service, exhorting and encouraging before prayer, and then praying with folks who came to the altar. I visited the sick and prayed and loved the family with all my heart. We are a small church of around 150, and we were who we had...who God had.

There are some stories I am not ready to tell, and there are some places of vulnerability in which I am not ready to be vulnerable. Perhaps those places will never be exposed because no one other than God is trustworthy enough to carry them, to hold them, as I do. Time will tell.

I am not telling you this story out of any resentment or anger. I am telling you so you can be on your guard, so you're not crushed if it happens to you—so you don't shrink back from the ministry God has called you to. And ladies, I am telling it so you don't fall prey to this type of judging and ruin someone else's life, ministry, or marriage. I don't have animosity. I have a broken heart. Do not be the one who breaks someone's heart. Who are you to judge God's calling?

Eventually twenty-five of our dearly loved folks left the church. It hurt our church deeply. It hurt my husband deeply. It crushed his spirit. There were other things that came into play, but the spark that flamed the fire was *a word whispered about my role in the church.* Gossip! Proverbs 17:9 says, *"He who covers a transgression seeks love, but he who repeats a matter separates friends."* And it certainly did. Yes, at the root was the opposition of a few to my role in the church, a role I didn't choose. A few folks walking in an authority that was not theirs, a coalition of a few who felt that they had heard from the Holy Spirit but that my husband, the pastor, had not.

I have a hard time trusting—not God—but people, perhaps because of the pain of my mother's desertion, or the pain of infidelity, or perhaps because so many friends moved on in their lives without me. I didn't trust in Frank's love for many years of our marriage. When he would tell me he loved me, I would always say, "I still don't believe it." Eventually, I did come to believe he loved me, but I still didn't fully trust him. There was always 2% of me waiting for the shoe to drop, waiting for something crazy to happen. Now, for me to trust anyone 98% was a miracle, but 98% is not good enough.

If you are standing in the path of a bomb, 2% of the radiation can kill you. I was still exposed to the radiation. Then, one Sunday morning, my husband called a special business meeting to address the rebellion in the room. He moved and spoke with the authority and anointing of the Spirit to protect the sheep of his flock, the flock God had charged him to protect. Some didn't understand, but *I* understood. I knew my husband, and I knew that day that he walked in a wisdom and manner greater than himself—greater than any of us. That day was the day I came to fully trust him. It was a hard day, but for me, it was a day of gaining 2%.

If you are a woman in the spotlight, speaking out, someone will not like it. But if you are where God wants you to be and doing what God wants you to do, then bow low and speak loudly. Don't shrink back. God will not forget you in the heat of the spotlight, either.

Frank and I had longed for a ministry we could do together and not be separated all the time, and God answered. We didn't know how hard it would be. It's still hard, and it still hurts, but we wouldn't change a thing. I am his helpmeet. He trusts in me, and I fully trust in him. And we trust in God. What a lavish reward. Our church is alive and well and strong and growing. We didn't shrink back.

I challenge you today to stand back and assess your household—assess your relationship with your husband, with your friends, with your family, and especially with God—and begin to put in order those things that are out of order. Go to the Lord and let Him know that you are willing to surrender control of your life to Him. Yield yourself to His will. Allow the truth that I have shared with you to change you. Total surrender brings total peace. Take on the mind of Christ and be transformed, not conformed. You will experience a new vitality in your relationships and a new confidence in who you are. God's Word says He will make your feet like hinds' feet and take you to the high places. He will *never* forget your name.

My prayer is that each of you will be so alive in your relationship with Christ that there will never be a hindrance that blocks the power of Holy Spirit; that the line of communication will flow freely; that there will never be a time when you ask, "God, where are you? Father, who is going to minister to me?" I pray there will never be a time when you will not hear His voice and know His complete will and purpose for your life. You will never be without His strength and His joy to see you through the intimate struggles of life and the public struggles of ministry, and I pray that you will never be without humility when He propels you to the spotlight.

Go to the high places. Rise above your circumstances. I am not alone, and neither are you. There is someone who wants to minister to you. Open your heart and receive it.

God bless you all today with a new hope, a new trust, and a renewed faith. May your marriages be filled with excitement, with passion, and with love, and your lives full of every good and perfect gift.

And may your very existence be proof of God's existence.

"Remember these, O Jacob, And Israel, for you are My servant; I have formed you, you are My servant; O Israel, you will not be forgotten by Me!" Isaiah 44:21

CHAPTER NINE – MEET BEVERLY LAHAYE

In a court of law, the most articulate, learned attorney would face defeat unless he or she could offer evidence to support their case. If that attorney is to win over the jury, he or she must have proof. So it is with most of us. Generally, we do not take things at face value or hearsay but demand all claims be validated by proof. If we are going to try a new product or program, we want to be sure of its success before we invest our time and money. Today, we may simply scan Yelp for reviews…but Yelp doesn't post reviews on the Bible. Maybe it should. Maybe *we* should.

I have challenged you to go against the grain of a society that promotes self-exultation, and live a life yielded and submitted to God. Not to proclaim your independence, but to announce your co-dependence on Christ. To have self-control, instead of expressing yourself. (Wow, don't let this book fall into the wrong hands, or we might just see a riot, or *maybe we could see a revival!*)

Now let me substantiate my claims. Being the intelligent audience that you are, I knew I would have to produce proof if I was going to convince you to put these truths into practice. How better to prove a point then by the testimony of a credible witness? And so, let me introduce you to one of the most successful, dynamic

Christian women in our world today—*a very credible witness*—a woman who truly understands God's divine order. Twenty-six years ago, in November of 1993, I had the privilege of interviewing Dr. Beverly LaHaye—an interview that clearly demonstrated God's faithfulness in fulfilling His promises. Today she still stands as a witness to the truth that if we trust Him and obey His commands, if we submit, if we live lives of humility, He will lift us to a place of honor. I was honored that she made time for me…but then again, that is who she is.

Ladies, meet Dr. Beverly LaHaye, founder of Concerned Women for America (CWA). She originally intended CWA to be a local group when she launched her first meeting in 1979 in San Diego, California, but the group grew to a nationwide organization within two years, and she later moved its headquarters to Washington, DC. CWA was established as a women's public policy organization devoted to Biblical principles to counter the feminist movement. Dr. LaHaye once announced at a press conference: "This is our message: the feminists do not speak for all women in America, and CWA is here in Washington to end the monopoly of feminists who claim to speak for all women." CWA is still standing for public policies that uphold Biblical principles and fighting against those who intend to dismantle them. Her influence still stirs our hearts to carry the banner…to be women used of God.

MEET BEVERLY LAHAYE

Beverly was the wife of the late Tim LaHaye, a Christian minister and prolific author of the *Left Behind* series, and is a prolific author in her own right. *The Spirit-Controlled Woman,* was published in 1995, with many additional works following. (5)

THE INTERVIEW

Q. Is it important to be sure of God's calling?

A. I have always said, make sure if you are going to separate yourself from your family, that it is God's calling. If not, you are putting yourself in the danger zone without God's blessing. Once you have the assurance that is where God wants you, then there will be a peace that the family can draw on. If serving the Lord is your highest priority, then you will have that peace.

I remember many, many years ago, in the early days, when our children were still at home and I was actively mothering, that my husband would be gone holding a week-long meeting at a church or doing a family conference and something would always go wrong. The plumbing would break, or we would get an unexpected bill. It just seemed like the devil was constantly throwing these little obstacles in front of me while he was on the road, trying to trip me up, and cause me to be in a state of discontent and frustration.

I remember on one trip when the plumbing did go out, I was having a pity party, rehearsing how I was home alone trying to repair the house and take care of the four children while he was out "there". Well you know what I'm saying…I was frustrated. Then, about a week after he had returned home, I received a letter from one of the ladies who had been in his meeting. It said, "Beverly, I want to thank you for sharing your husband with others. I want to tell you what God has done in my life." She went on to say how God had got ahold of her and that she had come back to the Lord. She told of how she had confessed her sin and been restored. It was a marvelous story of repentance and transformation. She was thanking me for sharing my husband and being a part of bringing that change to her life. I felt so convicted that I had not willingly done that. I had not willingly shared my husband. I realized that I was every bit a part of that ministry even though I was at home having the plumbing repaired. I believe it was that situation, at that instant, that I began to plan a program for my children while their father was gone. Every day we would have a new report on what victories he had had the night before, and how we were going to pray for him today. Each day we would have one specific prayer request that the children and I all shared together for their father, as he went about ministering. Whether it was, "Give him a new message today, Lord" or "Heal his cold." He had problems with his voice, so we would specifically pray for his voice. It helped us all feel a part of his ministry.

Q. Can you share with me how you maintain a close relationship with the Lord? Despite the circumstances, how can you keep your joy and continue to trust God?

A. When you're in the public eye, people tend to think that you don't have to go through trials and heartache. They might say, "She doesn't know how I feel, because she hasn't been there." I want to dispute that right up front. That just isn't true. I have the same disappointments, the same heartache, the same pain that everyone else has. But I also have the same God who has promised to walk with me through these painful areas of life.

One of the things I had to work on many years ago was the attitude of my heart. I found out that I could wake up in the morning and I could choose to be happy or I could choose to be sad and feel sorry for myself. The happiness that was long-lasting was based on my thoughts. If they were thoughts of negativism, complaints, and criticism, I could spend a whole day in that mode. Or, if I woke up and concentrated on the positive things and thanked God even for those things that I wouldn't have chosen, then I would be in a positive mindset for the whole day. All of us can develop a list of things that we are thankful for and focus on those things. We can choose to quit concentrating on the things that aren't going right, the things that aren't pleasing us. God is the one who is in absolute control when we are trusting Him and trying to walk in His will.

I learned a long time ago that it would be my attitude that would determine my accomplishments for that day. So, my prayer each day is, "Lord, give me the attitude that will help me accomplish all I need to do today to please you." I have learned that I can do everything today that is God's will for me to do. So when I go to bed at night, if I didn't get my long list of goals accomplished, instead of being depressed and blue and down in the dumps, I know that if my attitude has been right before the Lord, in submission, in prayer, and in total dependency, that I have accomplished everything that was God's will that I accomplish that day.

Q. Given the title of my book, *Who Ministers to Ministers' Wives*, who do you feel the minister is? Who is the one who sustains you and comforts you in times of trouble?

A. Well, before I answer that, I think ministers' wives need to be warned about the perception that we don't have problems. Being a minister's wife dedicated to serving the Lord doesn't mean we are exempt from the problems of life. Our children may cause us the same heartbreak. Our neighbors may do to us the same as they would to anyone else. But we know that we have a God who is going to walk with us through those problems. I think more than anyone else, ministers' wives need to be reminded of that. There are some who feel we are exempt from the troubles of life, so when they face trials, they wonder if God is displeased with them, if that's why He is piling all these things on them. No! He is not piling the things on us. However, He does want us to trust Him through the problems. The promise we should claim is, "I will never leave thee nor forsake thee." Even when things aren't going like roses, we can trust He is there with us. He says, "I'll not leave you. I will be right there with you." That's the comfort we must depend upon.

Q. Does God reward those who yield to Him? Has he honored your years of sacrifice?

A. The position I hold today is nothing I sought after. I was not looking for this. I was extremely happy being a mom and a grandmother and a pastor's wife. I could have spent the rest of my life doing that, but God had other plans. By trying to please Him and follow His leading, He has led me to where I am today. I have the total support of my husband. I could not do this if my husband was not one hundred percent behind me, encouraging me. I thought, *Isn't that interesting—that in the earlier years I was the one who stayed at home and prayed for him and encouraged him, and today the roles have changed.* Oh, he still has a great ministry, but now he has become my greatest supporter and prayer warrior. I am in an arena that if

God ever took His hand off, or cut off this limb I am out on, there would be nothing left. I am totally dependent every moment on His wisdom and His guidance, and my husband is my greatest backer on that. That's the unity in marriage. I gave to him and upheld him, and today my husband is upholding me. He gives the encouragement and support I need to be out on the front lines. You become a team. I think the ministry should always be viewed as a team. A husband and a wife teaming up together.

My role in Concerned Women for America (CWA) brings me a lot of recognition, a lot of negative recognition sometimes, but the Lord has taught me that it's not the recognition, whether negative or positive, but it's the fact that I want to make a change. I want to be an influence for good. I want to make a positive impact for Him.

I want to encourage you women coming along, you new moms, that we can make a difference in our society by standing strong and not compromising, not negotiating, but being strong in our convictions. If there was ever a time for Christian women, for ministers' wives to be strong in their faith and be willing to speak out on their convictions on Biblical principles, it is right now. The world is starving for someone of conscience, someone of conviction, to be an example…to make a stand. This is where the minister's wife can be a role model…by being a woman of conviction.

MEET BEVERLY LAHAYE

Thank you, Beverly, for sharing your thoughts with us. You are truly an example of a woman led by the Spirit of God. You are an example of how the blessings come through submission. The promise has been fulfilled—*Your works praise you in the gates.*

Although this interview was done twenty-six years ago, it still rings true today. We have a challenge, we have an example, and we have a minister within. Let us rise to the occasion, submit to God, follow where He leads. You will not be disappointed.

"Now may the God of hope fill you with all joy and peace in believing, that you may abound in hope by the power of the Holy Spirit." Romans 15:13

Chapter Ten – Make the Trade

If we lose our joy, we lose our strength. I know well from my own life that it's impossible to fully grasp God's goodness or glorify Him when in deep sadness. But I had no strength to overcome it. How can we do good works if *we* don't work? If our minds are broken, it's hard to tell others they can have the mind of Christ. If our hearts are broken, it is hard to tell others about the heart of Jesus, and if our spirits are crushed, it is hard to walk in the Spirit. We can barely get out of bed.

Proverbs 18:14 *"The spirit of a man will sustain him in sickness, but who can bear a broken spirit?"*

Proverbs 15:13 *"A merry heart makes a cheerful countenance, but by sorrow of the heart the spirit is broken."*

Every time I look in the face of women burdened with heaviness, with grief, with guilt, with sorrow, I can't look away. I know the look. I wore it for many years. I want to throw my arms around them and take it all away. I want to do for them what I wanted someone to do for me. I want to tell them my story. I want to tell them it doesn't have to be so hard. I want to tell them about Jesus and how He saved me, how He saved my life. I want them to know they can have JOY. I want them to see my JOY—the JOY of the Lord.

As I have relayed throughout this book, my life has been full of heartache, sometimes to the very point of wishing for death...but God saved me and lifted me out of my despair. I remember a night thirty years ago, just before Frank joined *The Sound*, when standing at an altar during a revival service I traded my sorrows for the JOY of the Lord. I went to the service mentally and spiritually weak, longing for more power to serve God better. I stood at my seat with my eyes closed during the altar call asking God to give me more power when someone put their hand on my head and said, "You are starving for more power." I didn't open my eyes. I rested in the words, knowing God had heard me. Later, as the altar call continued, a call was given for anyone who wanted more power to stand for God to come forward. I went forward. To my surprise, Frank came down from the platform and joined me, and two of my sons also came forward. We stood together along with thirty or so other precious people. I closed my eyes, again asking God for power to serve Him better, and once again, a hand lightly touched my head...and I felt the power. I cannot explain it. But, from that day to this, I have walked in that power. The power of the Holy Spirit became real to me that night. I don't know why, and I don't know what made that night different, but it was, and I was changed. Frank asked me a few days later what that night meant to me. Without hesitation, I said, *"It gave me a sound mind."* I have faced many trials since that night, but my faith has not been shaken. The power has not diminished.

The tormenting thoughts of suicide left me that night. I could say that no matter what comes, I know there is good on the other side, and I am still saying it.

I also relayed in previous chapters how God equips us for what is ahead, and I am a testimony to that. I have walked through the fire and not been burned, and through the floods but not overtaken. I stand strong and speak out about His unsearchable, undeniable, unchanging LOVE and MERCY. I speak out about the power we have to walk in JOY. I speak out about the miracles of God because I am one! I have shared several events of my life story with you to demonstrate the power and ministry of the Holy Spirit. Now let me end our journey together with a quick rundown of miracles not yet mentioned—the miracles that let me know that my Father knew me when I was formed in my mother's womb. He destined me for good works. He destined me for *this* work.

- As an infant, the doctors told my parents that I would not survive. I had three kidneys that were not functioning properly, a deformed spine, missing my C3 vertebra, and was unable to digest food. They took a picture of me in the hospital, thinking it would be the last. *(I keep the picture as a reminder.)* **I lived against all odds.**
- When I was five, I couldn't eat anything without throwing up. The doctors once again told my parents I wouldn't make it. As a last resort, they did an exploratory surgery and found numerous

tumors in my abdomen blocking organs from functioning normally. They cut them out. **I lived against all odds.**

- At the age of nineteen, I lost my peripheral vision and the ability to grasp and hold anything in my right hand. The initial test revealed an aneurism on the left side of my brain. The nurse told me I had to come to the hospital immediately and that I was scheduled to have an arteriogram the next morning to pinpoint the exact location to determine if they could operate. I chose to take what could be my last day on this earth and experience the city of Washington, DC with my friend. At the time I was not walking close to the Lord, but I prayed that night for Him to save me. I checked into the hospital early the next morning, with my friend Missy by my side. Having the arteriogram was the most excruciating pain I have ever experienced. But there was no aneurism to pinpoint. **The symptoms had left!**
- At the age of twenty-two, a cyst ruptured in my stomach. At midnight, with a 105° fever, the doctors did emergency surgery to save my life. The next morning, the doctor told me he saw an embryo. He told me I would live, but the embryo would not. I lay flat on my back waiting to miscarry. **Jay lived.**
- Also at the age of twenty-two, I was hit by an eighteen-wheeler going 80 mph. I was now three months pregnant with Jason. I lay paralyzed, waiting to miscarry. Within a week, the paralysis left. **I lived and Jay lived.**

- Two months later, I was in another severe car accident. I was now five months pregnant with Jason. I lay for a week, waiting to miscarry. **We both lived.**
- I'll bypass all the minor near misses and hospital stays and end with the most recent surgery. I mentioned I was born without the C3 vertebra, and with that, my head was gradually tilting left—today, about 3/4 of an inch—causing a lot of issues. In August of 2016, I went to a doctor in Houston to see if he could help me. He said my neck was like a rusty oil pan with rusty bolts and if he tried to fix it, it would crumble. So I headed to Austin to see the doctor who had done the first surgery, on my cervical spine, fifteen years earlier. He was also my friend. I had been his banker in 2002 – 2003 and had once taken a two-week vacation to work in his practice when his office manager unexpectedly quit. Now Dr. Spann was a miracle himself. Between my two surgeries, he had had a severe accident that left him a paraplegic. (*I know…you can't make this up.*) Years earlier I had gone to the hospital to pray for him. He was in a wheelchair with his C-spine fused. God gave him a miracle of healing. The "miracle doctor" was once again going to be my miracle. It didn't look good for me, but he said what he said the first time: "If you're game, I'm game." Sounds a little scary, right? I have to say, this time I was scared. The risk was real. He was going to fuse my whole C-spine together, from C1 to C7. The spine could easily be

compromised. If considering all that wasn't enough, the surgery would be in Austin! How was I going to pull that off? I pushed down the anxiety and fear and prayed for God's peace. I put it all in His hands and moved forward. God worked it out. Frank and I drove to Austin for a Wednesday dinner with all my sons the night before surgery. I figured, if this is it, I want it to be a memorable time with my boys. Frank got someone to cover for him for the Wednesday service, but he would have to be back in Houston and ready for Sunday. Given that I am writing this book, you know it went well. It was rough, and I am literally a "stiff-necked" woman (physically speaking,) **but I am walking and breathing and laughing and writing!** Frank traveled back to Houston late Friday night and as before God provided for me. My sweet friend Carol took time out of her life to drive up from Houston and stay with me in Austin until I could travel home. God is good!

So, I said all that to say this (to quote my husband from one of his sermons): *"If God has a purpose for you, you are invincible."* I believe I am invincible. I believe in miracles. Just the fact that you are reading this book is a miracle. I interviewed Beverly LaHaye twenty-six years ago for this book, and then life happened, and it lay dormant. Maybe I should say, God happened, and the book lay dormant. His timing is perfect. I became my own credible witness over the last twenty-six years. Frank is still serving in full-time ministry, and we are still standing to the glory of God. And only a miracle could have made it possible for me to reconnect with Mrs. LaHaye and keep my promise that I would not publish without her review. A phone call and a twenty-six-year-old letter made it possible. *God* made it possible.

"For with God, nothing is impossible." Luke 1:37

When we apply God's Word to our life, and stand in faith believing, there is nothing we can't achieve. NOTHING is too hard for God! When we recognize that we are no longer subject to Satan's defeating, destructive lies, we take them off like taking off a winter coat. We set aside the weights that so easily encumber us. We are lighter. Our sense of joy is awakened. We walk in a new light, illuminating the path for others. Like Paul, our pain becomes our testimony to the goodness and power of God. We delight ourselves in the JOY of the Lord, and His JOY becomes our strength. And with that strength, strong in our faith, we move mountains.

In September of 2018, I launched the inaugural *Make The Trade* Women's Conference at Freedom Fellowship Church. It was a big success! My heart was stirred by the response to the Friday night altar call as ladies came forward to trade their sorrows for the JOY of the Lord. God affirmed that the tug on my heart concerning the deep need for women to lay down their sorrows was *His tug*. I'll never forget how one of the attendees looked at me with tears streaming down her face, and said, "I get it!"

MAKE THE TRADE

It was a lot of work to pull off such an event, but the response made it worth it all. The next morning, my long-time dear friend Rosilyn Houston greeted our ladies with a powerful message of victory, affirming the message of JOY being our strength. She too has walked through fires and floods victoriously! I know it because we walked through some of them together. Our hearts were joined in 2005 when we found ourselves working together at BBVA Compass Bank in Dallas, Texas. When I called and asked her to speak, she didn't hesitate. Loyalty is a powerful thing. Roz is the highest-ranking female at BBVA in the United States, responsible for thousands of employees, and is a panelist on the *Propel* Women's Activate Conference, impacting thousands of women…and the list goes on. But she put her schedule on hold for two days to bring JOY to 100 ladies because I asked, and because God led.

The ladies came to the conference with sorrow but traded that sorrow for JOY. They wiped away the tears, looked to Christ, and looked to the future. They realized that the husband, or friend, or woman on the pew next to them, who didn't understand them, was loved by God. The hurt feelings were insignificant. What *was* significant was loving them. They left that Saturday afternoon with the power and JOY to glorify God, to show the world who they were…and who *He* is!

Join us for the next conference: http://www.freedomfellowshippearland.com/mtt-womens-conference .

My JOY will be complete as you trade your sorrows for the JOY of the Lord. We started with a hundred…I see thousands. Seventeen churches were represented…I see seventeen hundred. It will take us all to make it happen. We need a bright light to illuminate our dark world.

Fear in the present looks and longs for the future—*past joy*. Hope in Christ in the present looks to the future *with joy*.

"The joy of the Lord is my strength." Nehemiah 8:10

References — Online

(1) https://www.merriam-webster.com/dictionary/lowly

(2) https://www.cia.gov/library/publications/the-world-factbook/geos/us.html

(3) https://www.barna.com/research/new-marriage-and-divorce-statistics-released/

(4) https://www.thevintagenews.com/2016/09/05/priority-baby-boomers-nicknamed-generation-due-perceived-narcissism/

(5) https://en.wikipedia.org/wiki/Beverly_LaHaye

CHANGING LIVES WITH TRUTH IN STORY

Libby is changing lives with Truth In Story.

Be watching for the first book of her new fiction series…

THE PRAYER CARRIERS

THE RED WHISPER - Book One

www.ingramcontent.com/pod-product-compliance
Lightning Source LLC
LaVergne TN
LVHW090115080426
835507LV00040B/897